Doing it their way:
home-based education and autonomous learning

by Jan Fortune-Wood

The Educational Heretics Series

Published 2000 by Educational Heretics Press
113 Arundel Drive, Bramcote Hills, Nottingham NG9 3FQ

British Cataloguing in Publication Data

Fortune-Wood, Jan
      Doing it their way: home-based education and
      autonomous learning
      1.Home schooling
      I.Title
      371'.042

ISBN   1-900219-16-6

Design and production: Educational Heretics Press

Cover design by John Haxby, Edinburgh EH6 6QH

Printed by Mastaprint Ltd, Sandiacre, Nottingham NG10 5HU

Contents

Acknowledgements

Thanks are due to a great many people who helped with this book, both indirectly and directly. Thank you to Roland Meighan, who embraced this project from the beginning. Thank you to all the families who replied to my questionnaire. Some of you may recognise your words in the passages quoted, but all of the material was valuable in helping me to shape my thinking. A special thank you to Sarah Lawrence, who did not give up on me when I was resisting taking the leap into 'Taking Children Seriously'. Many, many thanks to Martine Archer, who graciously offered to proof read the text for me and really did a wonderful job. A very big thank you to my family, my husband Mike and my four children, who have not only ensured that I have had the time and space for writing, but who constantly provide me with the real motivation to live in an autonomy-respecting family. Finally, thank you to two people who encouraged me on my road of questioning everything; two people who were truly passionate about their own subjects; two great educators who nurtured in me my own thirst for education: thank you to John Smith and Lorna Clish.

Jan Fortune-Wood
September 1999

Part 1 Introduction:
The theory and philosophy of autonomous learning

Today's political climate is not largely one of educational experiment and diversity. The National Curriculum has become firmly lodged in people's minds as the blueprint of a proper education. The introduction of literacy, and now numeracy, hours in schools have gone a long way to standardising educational experience for the vast majority of children. In a political climate of paternalism and rigorous standardisation, home educating parents stand out as what Roland Meighan has called a beacon of 'trail blazing'. Amongst those who exercise their legal right not to delegate the parental responsibility for education to either the state or private institutions, autonomous educators are a small, but growing sub-set of people. Autonomous educators believe radically different things about learning and education. This book sets out to make their case and to do so particularly within the context of the British educational experience.

Whilst the thinkers who influence autonomously educating parents and children are, of course, international, there is a growing movement of people within the British Isles who question the logic of curricula, enforced teaching, adult-led subjects of learning and much more that goes with the mainstream package. Many of these parents have contributed to the later chapters of this book through sharing experiences of their own autonomous practice. Many others are attracted to the idea of autonomous, child-motivated education, but fear that it would result in a kind of stultifying nothingness or that it would take them beyond the boundaries of what is legally acceptable as an education. This book sets out to eradicate both of these myths and to make clearer the theory and practice which informs autonomous education.

Educational theory is not a homogenous or readily agreed upon body of knowledge. Over the course of the next three chapters, I aim to demonstrate that autonomous education is grounded in sound theory. This theoretical underpinning ensures that it is a valid and supportable lifestyle, which can be practised with confidence. I will begin with a brief overview of the thinking of those who have significantly influenced the trend to autonomous education, before moving on, in chapter two, to an examination of prevalent educational theories as they relate to autonomy. I will conclude part one of this book with a third chapter examining three broad schools of thinking within autonomous education; the theories of the natural child, 'unschooling' and non-coercion.

Chapter one

Focusing on theory

For those practising autonomous education, or 'learner-managed learning', their choice is not only an educational one, but also a moral imperative. Whilst any glance at the National Curriculum will readily show that autonomous education is not in the mainstream, none-the-less it does have a sound theoretical pedigree. We will see later that within the behaviourist-cognitivist-constructivist debate, autonomous learning finds a substantial theoretical underpinning in constructivist thinking. In this chapter I will begin by looking at a range of educational practitioners whose theories have given support to autonomous education.

Karl Popper's epistemology

Karl Popper is perhaps not best known as an unschooling theorist. But his theory of the growth of knowledge has contributed significantly to the *Taking Children Seriously* forum which is at the cutting edge of non-coercive educational and parenting philosophy. Popper himself proposed a new view of learning, no longer based on the inductive view of learning. In *The Myth of the Framework* he wrote for example,

> "The inductivist or Lamarkian approach operates with the idea of instruction from without, or from the environment. But the critical or Darwinian approach only allows instruction from within - from within the structure itself.

> "In fact, I contend that there is no such thing as instruction from without the structure, or the passive reception of a flow of information which impresses itself on our sense organs. All observations are theory-impregnated. There is no pure, disinterested, theory-free observation ...

> "We do not discover new facts or new effects by copying them, or by inferring them inductively from observation, or by any other method of instruction by the environment. We use, rather, the method of trial and the elimination of error. As

*Ernst Gombrich says, 'making comes before matching': the active production of a new trial structure comes before its exposure to eliminating tests." (*pp. 8-9)

On such a theory, extrinsic motivation is ruled out as a totally ineffective strategy for learning. Furthermore, Popper puts problem solving at the heart of learning,

> "The proper answer to my question 'How can we hope to detect and eliminate error?' seems to me to be 'By criticising the theories and conjectures of others and - if we can train ourselves to do so - by criticising our own theories and speculative attempts to solve problems'."
>
> (In Search of a Better World, p.48)

Sarah Lawrence has rightly pointed out that,

> "Unschoolers say that instruction from without is highly unlikely to address the real interests and concerns, (or 'problem situation', as Popper calls it), of the individual learner. How could one person's, (or one school's, or one government's), vision of What Children Need To Be Taught possibly bear any relation to an individual child's burning questions, problems, and interests? Is it likely that a lesson planned for several children, (or millions of children, in the case of a national curriculum), will answer any questions the child happens to have at that time?"

Lawrence goes on,

> "This idea of children as active, self-directing learners is implied by Popperian epistemology: the growth of knowledge proceeds through an active, creative, rational process of conjectures and refutations rather than passive reception of information. Popper does not just think that instruction from without is inefficient as a means of education, he does not believe that knowledge ever grows through passive reception of information. ... Children are not buckets into which we can pour knowledge. ... Children - human beings generally - are not passive learners. They do not learn by induction. They are active learners, and each person has his own unique problem situation. That is, at any given moment, each person has a unique set of interests, concerns, questions and problems, that he is actively addressing.

In 'How Children Fail', the unschoolers' guru, John Holt, writes about the effects of teaching on children. To put what John Holt said into more Popperian terms, the child subjected to externally-imposed instruction is much more likely to be engaged in solving the problem of how to survive questions from the teacher with the least possible embarrassment, or how to perform, than in learning the content of the lesson. Thus the problem the child is addressing - what the child is learning in that situation - is nothing whatever to do with the content of the lesson. The likelihood that the teacher-imposed lesson will answer any questions in the child's mind, or in any way relate to the problem situation the child had before the start of the lesson, is negligibly small."

> (Sarah Lawrence, an internet post to the *Taking Children Seriously* list 1.11.95 'Unschooling and Karl Popper')

John Holt – 'Leave them alone ...'

Holt is perhaps the best known theorist of autonomous education and, although he defined coercion more narrowly than do the proponents of *Taking Children Seriously*, he none-the-less left a wealth of valuable material to draw on. In *Instead of Education* he wrote,

"Next to the right to life itself, the most fundamental of all human rights is the right to control our own minds and thoughts. That means, the right to decide for ourselves how we will explore the world around us, think about our own and other persons' experiences, and find and make the meaning of our own lives. Whoever takes that right away from us, by trying to 'educate' us, attacks the very centre of our being and does us a most profound and lasting injury. He tells us, in effect, that we cannot be trusted even to think, that for all our lives we must depend on others to tell us the meaning of our world and our lives, and that any meaning we may make for ourselves, out of our own experience has no value." (p. 4)

Holt graphically described the effects on children of not being able to control their own minds in *How Children Fail*. In one example he described a child who became irrational and fearful in the face of constantly trying to survive in the school environment.

"I was wondering what he learned. Not much; he certainly didn't gain any insight into the property of multiplication in

which I was interested. All that he had to show for his time was the memory, of a long and painful experience, full of failure, frustration, anxiety, and tension. He did not even feel satisfaction when he had done the problem correctly, only relief at not having to think about it any more."

Holt noticed that the child, who could also be described as intelligent, was, *"... literally, scared out of his wits"*. Holt concluded, dismally, that he could envisage no life ahead for this child, and, most damningly, reflected,

"It is no accident that this boy is afraid. We have made him afraid, consciously, deliberately, so that we might more easily control his behaviour and get him to do whatever we wanted him to do." (pp. 64-66)

To the autonomous home educator this makes no sense whatsoever. The whole situation is artificial and damaging. The extrinsic controls on behaviour are fragile and unlikely to leave any intrinsic moral attitudes, whilst the quality of learning is pathetic and of no intrinsic value.

After spending some considerable time trying to reform the American schooling system with a concept of 'free' schools, Holt eventually turned to the concept of unschooling. In *Teach Your Own* (p. 229) he advised parents,

"I say, above all else, don't let your home become [a] miniature copy of the school. No lesson plans! No quizzes! No tests! No report cards! Even leaving your children alone would be better; at least they could figure out some things on their own. Live together, as well as you can; enjoy life together, as much as you can."

Holt also developed the theory that active teaching can do only harm. He began from observation of babies, who learn at an accelerated rate by a process of trial and error and who master such complex skills as walking and talking without any formal tuition. He concluded that learning is a natural feature of being human, and anything can be learnt, at any age, by the same means of trial and error. In *Learning All the Time* he wrote,

"... At any particular moment in their growth their minds are full of theories about various aspects of the world around them ... We cannot help these unconscious processes by meddling with them. Even when we are trying our best to be

helpful, by assisting or improving these processes, we can only do harm." (p.103)

It is certainly true that no-one knows what is going on inside the mind of another except the person in question. It is also the case that unwanted intrusion, in the form of irrelevant teaching or instruction, is more likely to damage than enhance thinking. But there is a danger in some of what Holt writes, of giving the impression that learning is an almost mystical, magical process which could proceed in complete isolation. This is certainly the impression Holt gives in *How Children Learn* when he is describing his own learning about the operations of a loom and his annoyance at other people's efforts to teach him. Holt proposed that his best chance of learning how the loom worked was simply in his ability to open up his mind and allow the solution to come to him intuitively,

"... as we drove ... a most extraordinary thing began to happen. I was not thinking about the loom ... But as we talked, a loom began slowly to put itself together in my mind. ... Suddenly, for no reason, the image of a particular part would suddenly appear in my consciousness, but in such a way that I understood what that part was for ... I had no reason to believe that other parts would later appear in the same way ... they did ... Some of what people had told me, trying to explain the loom, came back to me, and now I could see what their words meant." (p.176)

Whilst the growth of knowledge under an autonomous style is difficult to analyse, because of its creative and non-mechanical nature, I would contend that this does not consign it to the realms of the purely mystical and anti-rational. We will see later, however, that amongst those who advocate autonomous education, there is one school of thought which leans more towards Holt's notions of learning as a mystical process within a 'natural' child. Whether they lean towards the mystical or the rational, it is clear from the input of those parents who have contributed to this book that the parents of autonomously educated children are not negligent and blasé about their children's need for input. On the contrary, they are highly involved with their children in providing resources for educational discovery, though always in ways that respect their children's autonomy. Such parents do not meddle in their children's minds or force upon them unwanted information, but they are constantly available to share information and find new sources of information.

Whilst the process of conjecture and refutation that goes on in the mind of the autonomous learner is known only to themselves, and then often only on inexplicit levels of consciousness, this does not render the learning any less rational. Whilst, for those of us who would draw more heavily on Popper and on rational theory, Holt over romanticises the autonomous thought processes. Yet none-the-less provides a very thorough critique of compulsory school based education and the damage it inflicts on thinking. He similarly presents numerous examples of alternative, unschooling approaches which not only respect the individual child, but are demonstrably more effective educationally.

Ivan Illich – 'Deschooling'

Despite Holt's prolific output of books, for the most part, the assumption that school is an efficient means of imparting education still goes largely unquestioned in everyday culture. Yet it is an assumption that has been profoundly questioned for some time by concerned theorists. In the introduction to his book on deschooling, Illich wrote,

> *"... we have come to realize that for most men the right to learn is curtailed by the obligation to attend school ...*
>
> *"Universal education through schooling is not feasible. It would be no more feasible if it were attempted by means of alternative institutions built on the style of present schools. Neither new attitudes of teachers toward their pupils nor the proliferation of educational hardware or software (in classroom or bedroom), nor finally the attempt to expand the pedagogue's responsibility until it engulfs his pupils' lifetimes will deliver universal education. The current search for new educational funnels must be reversed into the search for their institutional inverse: educational webs which heighten the opportunity for each one to transform each moment of his living into one of learning, sharing." (Deschooling Society)*

For autonomously home-educated children those educational webs are found in their daily lives; in homes, freely chosen activities, museums, libraries, shops. Wherever there is conversation with those who feel a passion for their work and learning, each moment of living becomes a natural forum of learning.

Illich proposes various mechanisms for ensuring that all learners have access to such natural 'learning webs',

> "*Schools are designed on the assumption that there is a secret to everything in life; that the quality of life depends on knowing that secret; that secrets can be known only in orderly successions; and that only teachers can properly reveal these secrets. An individual with a schooled mind conceives of the world as a pyramid of classified packages accessible only to those who carry the proper tags.*" (p.76)

Illich proposes that this system should be replaced by access to what he calls 'channels' or 'learning exchanges', i.e. resources for real learning. He suggests that such resources are to be found,

> "*... in a world of things, surrounded by people who serve as models for skills and values. He finds peers who challenge him to argue, to compete, to co-operate, and to understand; and if the child is lucky, he is exposed to confrontation or criticism by an experienced elder who really cares. Things, models, peers, and elders are four resources each of which requires a different type of arrangement to ensure that everybody has ample access to it.*" (p.76)

Illich's utopia of access to educational webs involves such things as democratised resources and directories of peers with similar interests and elders with skills to share. Those educating children autonomously at home do not have such formalised access to educational webs, but none-the-less there are many informal networks of sharing resources, information, skills and interests. These include home education support groups such *as Education Otherwise* or supportive networks (including virtual communities) such as *Taking Children Seriously* or the UK Home-Ed support list. Illich believes that,

> "*Administrative, technological, and especially legal arrangements are required to set up such web-like structures.*" (p.78)

Most autonomous educators, however, would contend that autonomous education, whilst it is the best theory known to them, is not something which can be legally mandated and enforced; but it is rather a movement that proceeds by education, argument and example. In a post-modern society, one which is increasingly dependent on modern technologies, Internet communication and information, autonomous education is perhaps the most likely developmental outcome of an explosion of freely available information. It is this societal development and progression that is more likely to lend support to autonomous education than artificially established skills directories or legislation to democratise skill sharing. None-the-less, Illich's criticisms of the school system and his insistence on learning webs are remarkable and timely ideas which, in more informal ways, autonomous educators are already practising.

Throughout *Deschooling Society* Illich's stress is on the damage done to individual autonomy by institutionalising education.

> *"Many students, especially those who are poor, intuitively know what the schools do for them. They school them to confuse process and substance. Once these become blurred, a new logic is assumed: the more treatment there is, the better are the results; or, escalation leads to success. The pupil is thereby 'schooled' to confuse teaching with learning, grade advancement with education, a diploma with competence, and fluency with the ability to say something new. His imagination is 'schooled' to accept service in place of value ...*

> *"... institutionalization of values leads inevitably to physical pollution, social polarization, and psychological impotence: three dimensions in a process of global degradation and modernized misery." (p.1)*

In the parlance of *Taking Children Seriously*, coercion damage leads to irrational and entrenched thinking. The child's loss of control leaves painful experiences of unresolved conflict, which have to be managed by various coping strategies, which in their turn serve to shut down creative thinking in that area. Compulsory, extrinsically motivated education, is likely to kill or at least impair in significant parts, the very creativity which is at the heart of all true learning.

Alice Miller – 'For your own good'

Of course mainstream education does not purport to have irrationality and impaired creativity amongst its aims. Rather it sets out a range of learning outcomes which view the child as a product whose value can be added to. To this end schooling is ostensibly structured to maximise benefit to the child. Sadly, it is benefit according to someone else's agenda and congruent not with any individual's growth of knowledge, (except by random lucky accident), but with a pre-ordained and ever-changing prescription of what is supposedly best for someone else to know, learn and think.

Alice Miller has long been a rare voice in the field of psychology to recognise that deciding what is good for a child and then forcing this so called good on them by any coercive means possible is highly damaging to personal integrity and to rational thought. Miller defines abusive behaviour against children very broadly to include many of the more subtle forms of manipulation which children experience.   She posits that since there is a wide conspiracy to redefine this abuse as 'acceptable parenting' for the child's own good, the child, in order to survive, has no choice but to repress his or her feelings and idealise what is actually a painful situation. Miller concentrates on parenting rather than compulsory schooling in her defence of children and, most recently, has turned her attention to the campaign to having smacking made illegal. None- the-less, her theory that early childhood trauma of the widest kind leads to damage and destructive thinking, is a key one for many parents who aspire to autonomous education for their children. Amongst those parents who contributed responses for this book Alice Miller was almost universally cited as an influence on their educational philosophy in so far as she exposed the myth that coercion is for the good of the child.

John Taylor Gatto – 'Dumbing us down'

The system of institutionalised education does just what Miller most deplores on a massive scale. It decides for individuals what is in their best interests to know and think. One person who has done a lot to challenge the assumption that the institution knows best is the former New York teacher, John Taylor Gatto. Gatto believes adamantly that the state school system is designed to destroy individual thinking in such a way that mass schooling and education become inimical ends. Accepting an award as teacher of the year, Gatto argued,

> *"I am confident that as they [children] gain self-knowledge they'll also become self-teachers, and only self-teaching has any lasting value.*

> *"... Good schooling or bad schooling, it's all the same - irrelevant."*

(excerpts from 'I accept this award..' quoted at www.he2k-plus.co.uk, the web-site of the British conference, 'Home Education for the Year 2000 and After'.)

Gatto is convinced that schooling is based not on the aims of promoting thought and creativity, but rather has its roots in a Prussian model of pedagogy which was developed to ensure homogeneity and a biddable work-force. In his article, *'The Curriculum of Necessity or What Must an Educated Person Know?'*, he points out that one of the Harvard Schools, offering advice to prospective students, had cited real world experience as being more valuable than credentials, and had gone on to list qualities which related to independent thinking and autonomous practice.

Gatto goes on, however,

> *"I don't think we teach any of these things as a matter of school policy.*

> *"And for good reason, schools as we know them couldn't function at all if we did. Can you imagine a school where children challenged prevailing assumptions? Or worked alone without guidance? Or defined their own problems? It would be a radical contradiction of everything we've been conditioned to expect schools to do. If you want your son or daughter to learn what Harvard said was necessary, you'll have to arrange it outside of school time, maybe in between the dentist and the dancing lessons ... "*

Gatto's sweeping condemnations of the schooling system lead him to look at alternatives in delivering education,

> *"Schools as we have arranged them are bad places for children to grow up. I include the schools generally thought of as "good" in that indictment, and I would suggest to you this is sufficient explanation why two-thirds of a million families nation-wide have taken their children back from public authorities and are educating them at home. (Current US statistics. Statistics for the UK are uncertain, but conservative estimates vary between 20-40,000 families.) That number will surely double in the next five years unless restrictive legislation stops it. Kids educated at home are brighter and more impressively human than institutionalized kids, simply because they are allowed to learn free of bells,*

bogus experts, phoney sequences, endless interventions and similar junk."

Gatto goes on with a list of serious indictments against institutionalised learning, commenting that,

"... Grouping children by age, by social class, or standardized reading scores is an inherently vicious practice, and a stupid one besides if your aim is to develop the intellect. ... Still another thing that schools teach is the meaninglessness of everything except external reward and punishment. By bells and many other similar techniques they teach that nothing is worth finishing. The gross error of this is progressive: if nothing is worth finishing then by extension nothing is worth starting either. Few children are so thick-skulled they miss the point."

Gatto points graphically to what children lose when their autonomy is taken away,

"Suppose you had to submit its whorls and ridges to surgical alteration in order to meet some state standard of a politically correct fingerprint. Ridiculous, right? Then why not equally ridiculous that some stranger tells your kid what to think, when to think, how long to think, what to find important in the thoughts, etc.? I tell you as a teacher the mutilation from this procedure is long lasting and in most cases, permanent.

"We teach that human dignity, even in matters as basic as urination and the movement of one's bowels, is at the disposal of others. "Do you really believe your child is not damaged by this pornographic form of socialization?"

The schooling mentality is so entrenched in modern thinking, especially as it is passed down by politicians and a plethora of experts who 'know best', that it is commonly taken for granted that control, testing, standardised attainments, subject classifications, timetables, rewards, punishments and reverence of experts are not only necessary, but good for children's learning. Gatto effectively deconstructs these irrational assumptions and leaves in their place an opening that autonomous education can readily fill. Autonomous educators, like Gatto, are concerned to reverse the current trend of mass schooling. Gatto has his own utopia of schooling and has re-channelled his major energies into alternative schooling experiments, but he also recognises that the most radical and authentic education is taking place in the homes of home educators:

> *"There are many fine, tested, wonderful and inexpensive ways to inspire children to provide a first-class education for themselves, we all know a few of them. But whether it's going to be possible to get an education in the new schools of the year 2000 will depend on political decisions made by those who hold power in trust for all of us. Or perhaps I am wrong. Perhaps it will depend on defiant personal decisions of simple people, like the quiet revolution of the homeschoolers taking place under our noses right now which may be the most exciting social movement since the pioneers, not least because it is leaderless; a revolution in which our type of factory schooling has been treated as irrelevant, which it most certainly is. Starting as a skeptic, I have been visiting home schools all over the country for the past two years; starting as a skeptic, I came away feeling like Ezekiel when he saw the wheel."*

(Excerpts from *'The Curriculum of Necessity or What Must an Educated Person Know?'* by John Gatto are taken from www.he2k-plus.co.uk, the web-site of the British conference, 'Home Education for the Year 2000 and After'.)

Roland Meighan – 'Overcoming superstition'

That the institution does not know best was certainly a prevailing theme of the 1999 home educators conference organised by Malcolm Muckle, at which Gatto spoke. Whilst Gatto's experience is American, his criticisms of the effects of schooling are internationally applicable and are being voiced with equal rigour by British scholars. One of the foremost amongst these is Roland Meighan, of *Education Now* and *Educational Heretics Press*. Meighan has characterised home educators as trailblazers of the next learning system and has written a series of articles in *Natural Parent*, an alternative parenting magazine, to disseminate his ideas. In an article entitled 'Natural Learning' Meighan contends,

> *"Parents soon find out that young children are natural learners. They are like explorers or research scientists busily gathering information and making meaning out of the world. Most of this learning is not the result of teaching, but rather a constant and universal learning activity as natural as breathing. Our brains are programmed to learn unless discouraged. A healthy brain stimulates itself by interacting*

*with what it finds interesting or challenging in the world
around it. It learns from any mistakes and operates a self-
correcting process."*
(From the Roland Meighan column in *Natural Parent* no. 2
December 1997)

In another article, describing the visit of a student teacher to a home
educating family where children had been diagnosed as dyslexic,
but none-the-less, were all engaged in multiple learning contexts,
Meighan asks,

*"Has literacy, in the form of reading and writing, become an
obsession or even a superstition?"*

He goes on,

*"The time and effort spent on teaching reading also flies in the
face of the facts that it usually takes about 30 hours to learn,
provided that it takes place in a learner-friendly environment.
This figure comes from Paulo Freire's work with illiterate
peasants in South America ..."*

Meighan notes that modern technologies are quickly throwing into
question the assumed dominance of literacy. It is perhaps
interesting, if not ironic, to note that it is just at the point that the
need for literacy is declining, that the government has introduced
literacy hours. As Meighan puts it,

*"... the move from an era of the domination of print-based
literacy into a new era where oral literacy will be more
central, is already under way..."*
(Quotes taken from *Educational Heretics Press* web-site. A
shorter version of the article by Roland Meighan was
published in *Natural Parent* in February 1998.)

Meighan lays a great deal of stress on the rapidity of change and
uncertainty in the present educational climate and believes that this
gives home educators an edge since they are already accustomed to
the rigours of 'continuous adaptation'. In a situation where there is
no educational consensus Meighan also supports the notion inherent
to autonomous education that learning is not a matter only for
experts. He says,

*"There is another reason why parents need to become
researchers. A few years ago, a student on a Master Degree
in Education course became wearied by the constant*

procession of research studies presented week after week. He asked me to tell him what, in my opinion, all the studies told us in the end. I asked for time to think about it. Next week I gave a verdict. 'What they tell us,' I declared, 'is that we do not know how to do it. We do not know how to educate children in a complex and changing world. If we knew, we would not have to research it any more. All the research is doing is trying to find useful clues.'

"This statement still holds. But we do have more and better clues than before. But it means that parents do not have to believe overconfident teachers and educationalists, just as patients do not have to believe overconfident nurses and doctors. We can sift the evidence for ourselves ... Asking questions may lead to unexpected conclusions and actions. Those reluctant educational heretics, the home-schoolers, decided that they could make decisions based on their experience and the available evidence, that were at odds with 'professional' opinion. They may have even come to the same conclusion as George Bernard Shaw who proposed that 'all professions are conspiracies against the laity', well, some of the time anyway, if not most of the time in some cases."

(Quotes taken from *Educational Heretics Press* web-site. A shorter version of the above article by Roland Meighan was published in *Natural Parent* in March 1998.)

If following educational orthodoxy leads to little more than quasi superstitious belief in unproven experts, Meighan suggests that autonomous educators can look, instead, to a host of original thinkers who have themselves questioned the dubious link between schooling and learning.

"... when Mark Twain said that he 'never allowed schooling to interfere with his education', he drew attention to a number of propositions. One is that schooling and education are not the same thing, and can often be entirely opposed.

"Another is that your own private investigations, conducted in your own time and in your own way, can be valid education. Indeed, one of the reasons why schooling and education can be in opposition is that the questions and concerns of the learner can gradually become replaced by the official questions and concerns imposed by others and, even more oppressive, the officially approved answers."

(Quotes taken from *Educational Heretics Press* web-site. A shorter version of the above article by Roland Meighan was published in *Natural Parent* in March 1998.)

Meighan cites the leading educational superstitions of the present time as being literacy, Shakespeare, maths and handwriting. He points out that in each of these fields the proponents are driven by a question of fear,

"What if the learners do not choose to learn Mathematics?"

The answer, as Meighan points out, is simple,

"...the idea that we must all go through the Maths experience to identify those who are good at it and need it later for specific tasks, is about as sound as saying we must all study dentistry to enable some expert dentists to emerge. When I was learning Maths at school, then teaching it in school myself, and then watching my son learn it, the same heretical thought kept occurring, that surely there are better things we could all be doing than this."

At a point in time in which access to information is assuming gigantic proportions, and any enquiring mind can learn the contents of, say, a maths GCSE, in a fraction of the time it would take in school, from an interactive CD ROM, it is simply not sensible to claim that every child must plod through a given maths course. As Meighan says,

"... it was Paul Goodman, in a book that shocked people in 1962 entitled 'Compulsory Mis-education', who described mass schooling, including its imposed mathematics, as a mass superstition.

"The enthusiasts for imposing a curriculum on the learners are also worried by joined-up handwriting. 'What if the learners do not choose to learn joined-up handwriting?' I must admit to being much more worried if they do not develop the skills of joined-up thinking that learning logic encourages, but that is another issue. Perhaps more pain is inflicted on children in the joined-up handwriting pursuit than any other. Yet printers print in script because it is clearer."

(Quotes taken from *Educational Heretics Press* web-site, a version of which was published in *Natural Parent* in April 1998 as the Roland Meighan column entitled *The three myths)*

Meighan's exposure of the myths and superstitions of compulsory schooling supports the theory that not only should the content of education be whatever the child chooses, but also that the likely styles of learning to be found in autonomously educating homes are also more effective. In his discussion of learning styles he notes that the necessary styles of school based education are not likely to lead to effective learning.

> *"When I trained as a teacher I was introduced to two basic roles. One was that of crowd-control steward, since a great deal of time is spent dealing with large groups of conscripted learners. Conscripted learners, like conscripted slaves, are not likely to be automatically pleased about their enforced activity, and therefore need marshalling.*
>
> *"... The other basic role was that of crowd-instructor."*

Meighan proposes instead that three other learning systems are superior and notes that in each case there are other systems likely to be at work in home education, particularly where autonomy is valued. The first of these is 'purposive conversation'.

The second is that of teaching something to someone else, (with the learning experience being focused on the teacher rather than the instructed.) Thirdly, he suggests 'learning co-operatives' where democratic learning takes place between a whole group (or family). (Quotes taken from *Educational Heretics Press* web-site. This piece was published in *Natural Parent* in June 1998, as the Roland Meighan column, entitled 'The cop without a uniform'.)

All of these learning systems are present within autonomously home-educating families. Conversation is the single most important resource which children have in such homes and the greatest aid to their growth of knowledge. In an environment where control and instruction are paramount, conversation is at a premium and for some children access to purposive conversation is almost totally denied. Whilst there are always experiments in peer and group learning within schools, these in no way compare with the real life versions of children passing on valued skills and knowledge or groups of children or families learning as a co-operative unit. This is because the learning is intrinsically motivated by each individual within the group.

Autonomous education - a defensible view

There is no consensus as to what constitutes education and it is certainly the case that autonomy is not the flavour of the month in conventional educational thinking. But none-the-less, it can clearly be seen from the above range of theorists that autonomous education is not only a coherent, moral and defensible stance, but also one which is gaining ground and looking to the future of education, rather than harking back to some mythical golden era of standards.

Many of the tenets on which autonomy rests are negative ones; quite simply the school system is flawed and educationally suspect. But quite apart from the negative reasons not to school children in an attempt to educate them, there are enough positive reasons for following an autonomous approach.

Popperian epistemology fully supports the notion that extrinsic motivation and inductive reasoning are non-starters. Rather children, like all learners, are creative thinkers who proceed by a process of conjecture and refutation. This is a process which cannot be usefully speeded up or manufactured by artificial learning environments, but which must occur in the context of real problem situations relevant to the individual. On both moral and educational grounds, Holt supports the theory of autonomous education as being both that which respects the child as a real person with a right to his or her own thoughts and that which maximises the innate impulses to learn. In terms of structure and systems, autonomous education maximises children's opportunities to participate in what Illich calls 'learning webs'; that is, informal, but vital and real life contexts for learning, which are also the most likely to succeed in a post modern society, increasingly dependent on modern technologies and internet communication. Similarly, it gives full scope to Meighan's successful learning systems of conversation, one-to-one learning and learning co-operatives. In the psycho-therapeutic parlance of thinkers such as Alice Miller, it is autonomous education which allows for undamaged development. In the educational language of Gatto it is autonomous education which allows children to develop such abilities as being able to define problems, ask hard questions, work independently, argue coherently and use a wide range of thinking strategies.

If home educators are the trailblazers of the next learning system, as Meighan believes, then home educators who follow the principle of autonomy are at the spearhead of true education.   In case the support of major educational, moral, philosophical and psychological thinkers is not enough to convince, however, then let us turn to three prevalent theories of how we learn.

Chapter two

A place on the map

In this chapter I will set out the theory that education is not something that admits a single definition, but is rather a complex range of theories. I will go on to examine briefly three theories of education in relation to autonomous learning; namely, behaviourism, cognitivism and constructivism, before setting out a definition of autonomous learning and its key factor of intrinsic motivation.

A lack of homogeneity

That there is some standard definition of education is a myth too often promulgated by local education authorities and politicians. Despite popular misconceptions, however, the right not merely to home educate children, but to nurture the autonomy of that education is a valid, legal and sustainable one. (For a full legal account see Appendix 1.)

The word 'education' generally conjures up an image of some structured activity, which involves schooling. In fact, this image is only a flawed part of what is actually meant by a term on which there is, as we have already seen, no consensus. There exists a confusing plethora of educational theory, much of it contentious, but what the schooling mentality has tended to do is to narrow vastly the popular conception of what counts as 'proper education'. This book sets out to widen that mindset and, in particular, to place autonomous education on the map of the British Isles.

What is meant by the terms 'education' or 'learning' remains an open-ended question. Certain 'experts' are beginning to feel that they have some grasp of how people learn and particularly how children learn, but all are willing to admit that much more research is needed. Furthermore, it must always be remembered that even the best research can represent only the current best hypothesis available.

There is, as we might expect, an abundance of educational theory which does not support autonomous learning. But despite this there are theorists who are recognising that educational theory is not the scientific discipline which it sometimes purports to be. Bruce Goldberg, professor of philosophy at the University of Maryland and author of *Why Schools Fail*, has questioned the efficiency of curriculum in his article, 'Educational Theory' (January 15, 1997, www.cato.org/dailys/1-15-97.html). Goldberg recognises that the intention of curricula is to help children reach their maximum potential through courses of study, which claim to reflect best their mental development. He concludes, however, that in reality this is not what happens and that the whole notion of education as a 'science' is a myth. Goldberg notes that previous generations have fallen into the same error of basing educational theory on pseudo science and that there is a basic conflict between a mass system of education and the goal of maximising individual potential:

> *"The public school curriculum represents a group-orientated way of thinking about children, in which the interests, inclinations and talents of the individual child are treated as essentially irrelevant. It is not surprising that a system containing so much falsity, whose practices are so much at variance with its stated goals, is failing."*

Behaviourism

Nor does it appear to Goldberg that more recent so-called scientific thinking has benefited our educational theory. He points out that behaviourism has largely governed 20th century educational thinking, despite amounting to *"little more than grandiose claims without supporting evidence"*.

Although behaviourism began as a theory of psychology, its influence on conventional education has been marked. Positing, as it does, that, like animals, humans can be conditioned to react to stimuli or, as Skinner developed the theory, that behaviour is the result of having experienced certain consequences in the past, all learning becomes the result of external stimuli. On this theory the child has no mind, only a mechanical brain which responds to conditioning. It follows that neither can the child, (or indeed any of us), be responsible for actions, since actions are simply inevitable responses to external stimuli. Thus education becomes a process of manipulating behavioural outcomes; controlling learning by rewards and punishments. Behaviourist educational theory is characterised by such things as repetition, sequencing tasks in small, concrete and progressive stages, (Kumon maths courses for example), using negative reinforcement or rewards.

Working with behaviourist theory, learning is passive and knowledge is an absolute given. It is a theory which may produce automatic responses, but robs the learner of any flexibility or creativity. If the correct cue is not present, the learner will not know how to act. She/he becomes little more than an automaton; an outcome that may be considered desirable in limited authoritarian environments, but which ill fits children to cope in a fast moving, flexible world. Such thinking reduces human beings to mere products, totally demeaning their moral and creative status.

Cognitivism

Of course behaviourism is not the only learning theory that pertains in structured, formal learning environments. Cognitivism has also had some impact, allowing learning environments to provide a breadth of activities and content, so that students can customise their own learning within the framework of the larger aims and objectives of the curriculum. On this theory, children are encouraged to be active participants in their own learning and their role in being able to process and retrieve what is learned is given value. Cognitivists are particularly concerned with the mental processes of the learner and allow for learning that involves abstract reasoning, creative problem solving and complex information processing. Cognitive theories of learning are more likely to take account of individual learning styles and to encourage discovery. The overall choice, however, of what specific information should be learned and input into the student minds remains with the teacher or, in the case of a national curriculum, with the government. Knowledge is still a given body of absolutes. Learning is still basically seen as the transmission of ideas and consistent behaviour and the curriculum is delivered with the assumption that it is a consistent, balanced menu of educational necessity for life. As Goldberg points out, however, quoting David and Micki Colfax,

> "The ... curriculum - which embodies, at least theoretically, what is to be learned and when - is in fact nothing more than a hodgepodge of materials and assumptions resulting from the historical interplay of educational theories, political expedience, education fads and fashions, pretensions to culture, demagoguery, and demography. It is by no means, as the professional educators would have it, a coherent course of

study; or, as the more pretentious among them would have it, a distillation of our common culture.

"For those concerned with autonomous education, what is most disturbing about the behaviourist or cognitivist assumptions behind curricula is their complete disrespect for the individual child. One system does not suit all children or even many children, in focussing on educating children as though they were some kind of homogenous group the skills, and aspirations of individuals are trampled on and ignored."

Goldberg concludes,

"An education that would benefit an individual child, any individual child, would begin with an understanding of the interests, drives and aptitudes of that child. The grand plan of educators begins at the wrong place - with their goals for all. Those goals are supported by nothing but pseudoscience and rhetoric about elevating the spirit. Children then fail by not meeting the expectations of the 'experts' and their designs. But it is not the children who are failing - it is the experts who are failing to meet the children where they are. We will have better schools when we fit education to the child rather than the other way around."

Autonomous educators would conclude even more radically that we will have better education when we move entirely beyond the notion of schools which provide a pre-set agenda of transmissive education, into learning which is centred in the individual and motivated only by the learner.

Constructivism

One educational theory, which does support such goals, is that of constructivism. Constructivism develops cognitivism in order to place the learner centre stage as the creator and processor of the learning. The learner defines the educational environment with the teacher or instructor in a facilitating role. John Dewey, whose thinking influenced this school of thought up to 1950, placed an emphasis on individuality and creativity. Similarly another proponent of this school, Knowles, talks about self-directed learning, active and experiential learning environments. Knowles also saw instructors as facilitators, guides or resource people. Knowles, however, applied his thinking only to adult learners, stopping short of thinking that children might deserve such respect and autonomy. Despite this short-sightedness, constructivism does give us a more useful working model. Knowledge is not handed on as a given body of absolutes, but is constructed by the individual and fallible. Learning is based around problem solving in which the learner can construct his/her own reality. The learner thinks like an expert, starting from the problem, story or case before him or her and using a real-life framework to interpret multiple realities.

In too many educational circles it is taken as self-evident that whilst adults can and even should control and direct their learning, children must be directed from outside. Also, that whilst adults can make choices which maximise the growth of their knowledge, children need to be channelled along set courses without which they would inevitably end up ignorant and incapable. Such assumptions are not based on sound reason. Children lack experience, certainly, but it is not logical to deduce from this lack of experience that they therefore lack the rational and volitional qualities to make good choices about their own life and learning. Sadly, it is often rather the case that our wealth of experience as adults can be the very source of irrational theories about aspects of life and learning. For example, an adult who needs to learn new patterns of eating often has a wealth of unhappy experiences around food in his or her past. Experience is not the basis of reason, and lack of it should not be used to justify taking educational autonomy away from children, but merely offered as a possible guide and resource as children make their choices. This is not a new proposition, but it is one that has remained outside the mainstream, as we can see by looking back to William Godwin in *The Enquirer* in 1797,

> *"In what manner would reason, independently of the received modes and practices of the world, teach us to communicate knowledge? Liberty is one of the most desirable of all sublunary advantages. I would willingly therefore communicate knowledge, without infringing, or with as little possible violence to, the volition and individual judgement of the person to be instructed. If a thing be really good, it can be shown to be such. If you cannot demonstrate its excellence, it may well be suspected that you are no proper judge of it. Why should not I be admitted to decide, upon that which is to be acquired by my labour?*

> *"According to the received modes of education, the master goes first and the pupil follows. According to the method here recommended, it is probable that the pupil should go first, and the master follow.*

"This plan is calculated entirely to change the face of education. The whole formidable apparatus which has hitherto attended it, is swept away. Strictly speaking, no such characters are left on the scene as either preceptor or pupil. The boy, like the man, studies, because he desires it. He proceeds upon a plan of his own invention, or which, by adopting, he has made his own. Everything bespeaks independence and equality. The man, as well as the boy, would be glad in cases of difficulty to consult a person more informed than himself. That the boy is accustomed almost always to consult the man, and not the man the boy, is to be regarded rather as an accident, than anything essential. Much even of this would be removed, if we remembered that the most inferior judge may often, by the varieties of his apprehension, give valuable information to the most enlightened. The boy, however, should be consulted by the man unaffectedly, not according to any preconcerted scheme, or for the purpose of persuading him that he is what he is not.

"There is reverence that we owe to everything in human shape. I do not say that a child is the image of God. But I do affirm that he is an individual being, with powers of reasoning, with sensations of pleasure and pain, and with principles of morality; and that in this description is contained abundant cause for the exercise of reverence and forbearance. By the system of nature he is placed by himself; he has claim upon his little sphere of empire and discretion; and he is entitled to his appropriate portion of independence.

"Violate not thy own image in the person of thy offspring. That image is sacred. He that does violence to it is the genuine blasphemer. The most fundamental of all principles of morality is the consideration and deference that man owes to man; nor is the helplessness of childhood by any means unentitled to the benefit of this principle."

Reason is not an adult commodity that comes as the distillation of years of experience. It is an attitude that holds that problems are soluble, that mistaken ideas can be dropped and replaced and that criticism and the presence of competing ideas are helpful in reaching new conjectures. It is this rational process of conjecture and refutation that leads to new knowledge, and such learning demands an openness that children, rather than adults, often possess more abundantly.

Behaviourism, cognitivism, constructivism and the autonomous learner

The educational theories of behaviourism and cognitivism are clearly theoretically and morally insufficient as bases for autonomous education. Passive learning, whether based on crude rewards and punishments or on much more subtle manipulations, is not a basis for real motivation or for learning that will produce creative, flexible thinkers. Attention to learning styles that, none-the-less has a set agenda in mind, is disrespectful of the autonomy of the individual and unlikely to provide coincidentally the most appropriate learning for any given individual. Constructivism, when it is not narrowly applied only to adult learning, has more to commend it. Autonomous education is most likely to proceed where conjecture and refutation are welcomed.

It is interesting to note, however, that even where the operative theory of learning is totally flawed we will sometimes find the autonomous learner thriving. This can be explained, since what matters above all else is that the learner is intrinsically motivated. A child in a behaviourist-style classroom with no choice but to be there, is likely to fair badly. Even if he learns the lessons 'well' in order to survive or function he is unlikely to retain the learning long term and is highly likely to have his thought processes damaged along the way. By contrast, a child who has chosen to learn a martial art or who has chosen to be part of a scout troop, may well do a lot of learning in an otherwise coercive environment, simply because she/he is in control of being there, and is choosing the environment for his or her own ends. Behaviourist and cognitivist theories of education are poor paradigms for an autonomous education, but that is not to say that the autonomous child can never use these environments. The ability to stay or go and the source of the motivation are always what distinguish true autonomy.

As an overall paradigm, the constructivist theory of learning is more supportive of an autonomous style of education. In this theory, as we have seen, emphasis is placed on the learner and it is the learner who interacts with problems to construct his/her own solutions and ideas. The autonomy and initiative of the student is a given factor, and learning is something which takes place in the learner's mind rather than being transmitted from the outside. Conjecture and refutation are essential features of learning and children are given the opportunity to build on earlier ideas and knowledge. The emphasis of this theory is not on the teaching, but on the learning, and the process of learning is more important than an end product.

The constructivist theory of learning is also more likely to operate well in real life situations. Of course, the autonomous educator still has to adapt the theory to suit true autonomy. Within the classroom constructivist thinking may sometimes be used within a discipline, for example craft, design and technology, to allow the children to explore and construct their own hypotheses. This is being done, however, within the parameters of the children's compulsory attendance. There is the assumption that a certain subject defines the boundaries of what can be explored and the language of assessment of what is being learned will not be far away. (See chapter 7 for a full discussion of autonomy and evaluation.) None of this would be typical of an autonomous learning environment where the child is free to be part of an activity, group or individual pursuit as she/he desires and chooses; where possible avenues of exploration are suggested but never imposed and where learning is not something which constantly needs its temperature taken.

Autonomy and intrinsic motivation

Autonomy is the right of self-government and free will. Education is the process by which we develop intellectual potential and foster the growth of knowledge. Education relies on a rational development of conjecture and refutation. Autonomous education is simply that process by which knowledge grows because of the intrinsic motivation of the individual. In fact, the core to understanding autonomous education is in understanding the absolutely fundamental and unshakeable role of intrinsic motivation. It is quite common to find autonomy juxtaposed with other educational concepts in order to attempt to denigrate and stereotype the theory. It is not uncommon to hear that an autonomously educated child is effectively considered to be barred from ever sitting an exam or gaining a qualification; from ever learning anything which involves specific teaching; or from ever achieving certain kinds of academic knowledge. All of these suppositions are false. The one thing that is always inimical to learning in the sense that autonomous educators understand it is extrinsic motivation, that is, coercion. It might very well be that a number of children will not choose exams or qualifications as the means of forwarding their education, but it will be just as true that others will autonomously choose this route for their own intrinsic ends. It will certainly be the case that 'teaching' is often a less efficient way of enabling and is sometimes totally incompatible with learning. But it will also, on some occasions, be useful to the autonomously educated child where it is a self-chosen route, for example in learning to drive a car. Neither does autonomous education preclude gaining complex academic knowledge. It is not lack of structure or activity that characterises autonomous education, but simply the source of the motivation.

Intrinsic motivation has to be just that. J.P. Raffini has recently published a book entitled, *150 Ways to increase intrinsic motivation in the classroom*. The title is a contradiction of what autonomous educators mean by intrinsic motivation. The only way to increase this in the classroom would be to allow all the children who do not want to be there to leave and then to facilitate those remaining, (if any), in pursuing their own learning independent of subjects, timetables and curricula.

One person who has grappled extensively with the notion of extrinsic and intrinsic motivation is Alfie Kohn, in his book *Punished by Rewards*. In a conversation with Ron Brandt, editor of *Educational Leadership*, Vol. 53, No. 1 September 1995, Kohn argued that both rewards and punishments are manipulative. They destroy the potential for real learning, whether it is punishments that come in the guise of so-called logical consequences, or rewards that use things that people value as levers. Kohn cites social psychology as supporting his position that rewards actually decrease interest in the thing the person is engaged in and will tend to cause the task to be done less well. Kohn is also very wary of confusing motivation with mere compliance. Kohn is still, however, advocating a form of motivation that can work in compulsory classrooms. He wants lessons to be presented in child-centred language and experience, but does not fundamentally question that there is a curriculum that must be got through. He talks of the three Cs; interesting content, a safe community and choice, (by which he means input into how and why and what is being done). But this does not go all the way to meeting the demands of truly intrinsic motivation. Intrinsic motivation requires that the content is just the content which the child wants to engage in for her/his own reasons. The environment is one which the child chooses to be in and can leave, and that choice is not about being 'listened to' before a lesson proceeds anyway, but is genuine and unrestricted. Intrinsic motivation requires the freedom of self-government.

On the other hand, self-government, free will and intrinsic motivation are not co-terminus with neglect. To claim that children deserve their autonomy is not to leave them to it without any help or input, without any sharing of information or experience, as I will argue more fully in the next chapter. Children are natural learners, in the sense of being born as rational, creative thinkers with unimpaired minds. Whilst coercion destroys that natural learning ability, parents (and other trusted adults) still have an enormous role to play in helping children to achieve their ends and in introducing children to a wide range of possible interests. A child who is never forced to learn any academic subject still stands every chance of gaining academic knowledge if this is what he or she desires, but a child whose parents never engage with him/her will be severely hampered in gaining any kind of knowledge. Autonomy is not neglect. Neither, as I will argue more fully in chapter three, is autonomous education some mystical process that just happens. It may certainly be difficult fully to analyse in that it is a creative, unpredictable and non mechanical process, but it does not advocate abandoning children to their own devices. There is a world of difference, though, between engagement and manipulation; between being a valuable resource and a source of unwanted and unnecessary instruction. But finding the line where there is engagement and information sharing is an important factor in autonomous education.

Chapter three

Autonomously educated children

What we can certainly conclude from the brief survey of theories of education above is that autonomous education is a theory able to take its place amongst the many competing definitions of education. Autonomous education can draw widely on the constructivist theory of learning and the autonomous learner can employ any number of learning environments, although the key always remains the learner's ability to follow his/her own intrinsic motivation. Furthermore, as we have already seen, autonomous education can draw on a wide range of diverse thinkers for support; from Popper to Holt, from Miller to Illich.

Many parents feel that thinkers across a wide spectrum have influenced their belief in autonomy as the foundation of education. But amongst those who have taken this route there are three broad ways of looking at children which vastly influence the 'flavour' of the autonomy. The first two of these, I would argue, ultimately place boundaries around autonomy which will inevitably sabotage the most creative and rational thinking. All of these routes, however, undoubtedly go a very long way to at least fostering a culture of questioning and self motivation.

Natural and mystical

The 'leave them alone' approach of John Holt hints at a view of children as natural learners in a sense that is not altogether congruent with rational explanation. One parent talks about,

> *"Trust in an innate desire to learn, and in the child's innate, unconscious methodology, which we do not have to understand, but know it is a more accurate theory of learning than anything known to adults."*

Whilst rationalists might agree that we cannot second guess the processes of another's mind they would not go so far as to attribute mystical processes to them. Yet amongst those who espouse autonomy in education there is a very definite school of those who eschew rationalism and intellect in favour of instinct and intuition. The best known and most widely quoted guru of this approach is Jean Liedloff, author of *The Continuum Concept.* Liedloff spent two years living with an effectively stone age tribe of Yequana Indians in the South American rainforest before writing her influential work. She sees the Yequana as models of what it means to live in harmony with nature, one another and our children. The reason for this, Liedloff believes, is that the Yequana continue to have the same experiences of life in their emotional, mental and physical development as the human species would have had during our process of evolution. Whilst this includes parenting styles which are common to many who adopt alternative lifestyles, such as carrying small children, co-sleeping, breastfeeding and responding quickly to babies and children's needs, it also contains a level of coercive expectation which would not hold across the whole spectrum of autonomous education as it is practised in Britain.

Working with the continuum concept, children are responded to, but should never be the centre of attention. Liedloff completely opposes child-centred learning and development. Instead, she believes, adults should go about adult-centred tasks with the children as observers who will naturally join in as their age and ability allows. In this life apprenticeship Liedloff observes that very young children soon develop a strong sense of adult expectation and are obedient, quiet or even silent in adult company, conforming totally to the prevailing culture. Whilst Liedloff admires the undoubted harmony and apparently happy obedience which this results in and whilst she sees children's imitation of and respect for elders as both natural and fundamentally 'right', she fails to have any critique of this culture, instead romanticising Stone Age humanity as the pinnacle of evolution.

Liedloff's observations are far from neutral. The Yequana are a stone age subsistence culture. Whilst we may have much to learn from any given culture, the Yequana's adult-centred existence which children observe before imitating is a necessarily simple one in which the strictures of survival pre-dominate. Autonomously educated children in the developed world cannot so simply observe the whole of adult life at a glance before slotting into place. Yet Illich's concept of learning webs certainly does allow for greater flexibility in children learning alongside practitioners in various fields. Where survival is not a key issue many other autonomous educators would argue that child-centred, as well as adult-centred, learning environments are a mark of not just physical, but moral progress.

Liedloff extols the harmony of the Yequana, but never questions the morality of obedience and conformity nor the rigid elder/younger and male/female hierarchies that this maintains. In such a conformist culture, there is a remarkable lack of creativity. The tribe continues to solve the same problems in the same ways. Such a static lack of problem-solving, of conjecture and refutation is deeply conservative and stifling to the kind of autonomy that we see arising from Popper's epistemology.

There is within the continuum concept and within educational theories that root themselves in it, a strong anti-intellectual, and anti-rational strand. Liedloff herself talks about 'the dangerously ignorant hands of the intellect'. Whilst always being careful to own that we cannot know the rational processes of another's mind, and that many of these processes are not within conscious cognisance, it none-the-less remains unwise to base education and decisions for life on instinct. Instinct is not a pointer to some sacred mystical core of true humanity, but merely an indicator of previously evolutionary necessary responses. Whilst some of these may still have relevance, there is nothing unnatural or artificial about using intellect and reason to further that process of evolution.

Being allowed to develop naturally can sound so like being free to develop autonomously, but the two are not the same. Natural development is actually strictly controlled according to a preordained agenda of what it means to be 'natural', whereas autonomy has no agenda. 'Rightness' and 'naturalness' are not epithets that can ultimately hide the coercive nature of any education which is based on Liedloff's theories. Projecting any 'mystical', 'unspoilt' qualities onto children is ultimately demeaning. It traps children in an adult, romanticised fantasy of what it means to be a child. This is not autonomy.

Another danger of thinking that the learning process is in some way mystical or natural is that it may tend to encourage neglect. If parents seriously believe that children will not touch sharp knives because they are innately self-protecting or that complex theories of mathematics arise from the world as if by magic, then they are unlikely to feel the need to engage with children and constantly to share good information with them. Of course children are not innately self-destructive and can work out complex theories, but that is not to say that input is of no value provided it is welcomed and respectfully delivered.

In practice few, if any, parents who advocate autonomous education and who in some measure subscribe to the mystical, natural view of the child would be so neglectful. The parent quoted above who spoke of the child's innate, unconscious methodology also added,

> *"Our 'theory', if you can call it that, is that a child naturally wants to know about the world around them with a real passion which it is our business not to dull, but to feed where appropriate with information, resources, our interest and engagement with them, and exposure to new aspects of the world."*

Clearly such parents are highly engaged, but none-the-less arguments for leaving the natural child alone open up the danger of laissez faire, neglectful parenting, as Naomi Aldort illustrates in her web site article for the Natural Child Project, *Getting Out of the Way*. Speaking of her children as models of 'good' behaviour, she notes that the discipline comes from the parents' restraint in getting involved,

> *"We do not, however, meddle in their play, their learning, their creativity, or any other form of growth."*

Whilst Aldort, who recognises Jean Liedloff as a major influence, rightly criticises narcissistic tendencies in parents to 'show off' their children and whilst she correctly eschews manipulation based on rewards, she also goes much further,

> *"Only as we make a concerted effort to get out - and stay out - of our children's way do we discover the wonderful truth: the magic is already in our children, ready to unfold in its own way and in its own time.*
>
> *"Nearly every child comes to life equipped with a self that is capable of blooming to capacity. Unhindered in its growth, this self will lead the child to skills and knowledge and, in the process, self-actualization. We have no right to attempt to control the direction of this growth. Instead of training our children through various forms of intervention to fit our vision for them, we need to train ourselves to respect nature's creation and to safeguard its full, authentic bloom.*
>
> *"Indeed, the end result we are looking for - an able, highly self-esteemed, creative, curious, and responsible human being*

- is already observable in a two-year-old child. Allowed to put these gifts to use in a self-directed, self-trusting way, the youngster will develop capabilities while enhancing these desirable qualities. Maturation will then come as an authentic expression of the self, rather than as an appeasement to parental authority and other forms of domination.

"Getting out of the way gives us an opportunity to become curious observers. At the same time, it frees us of power struggles and initiates an approach to parenthood that is infinitely more enjoyable and fulfilling. I know of no more interesting, engaging, fascinating, and glorious 'entertainment' in life than watching children unfold freely."

On the face of it this sounds like autonomy, but it is not, because it comes with an agenda and with a fixed product in mind, namely a well-behaved (by the parent's lights) child who fulfils a list of product specifications based on an idealised understanding of what is natural to human nature.

Unfortunately, what is defined as 'natural' can too easily become a replacement for curricula. It might, for example, be that the child is free to develop, but it is expected that the natural, magical child will choose sanctioned foods, play with wooden toys, avoid arcade-style computer games, television and gun play. Whilst these areas are not ones which would conventionally be considered to be central to autonomous education, real autonomy does demand that intrinsic motivation is essential for all learning.   Limiting intrinsic motivation by any means, however subtly communicated, limits and severely hinders or damages thought processes. The coercion is not always so thoroughly applied; it might manifest in only one or two areas of thinking, perhaps, for example, a ban on gun play and restricted TV, or license to eat sweets, but not meat. Whatever the specific agenda and however subtly imposed, 'living naturally' will undoubtedly have some controlling effects which will tend to diminish the positive benefits of autonomous education. This is an issue to which we will return when examining the impact of overall lifestyle on autonomous education in chapter six.

Those who begin by practising attachment parenting, (breastfeeding on demand, family bed, etcetera.), and who take their initial inspiration from Liedloff, or from British proponents of her work such as Deborah Jackson in her books *Three in a Bed* and *Do not Disturb,* will often practice a significant degree of autonomy in their educational style as home educators. They contribute enormously to the range and diversity of educational practice and experience amongst home educators and most certainly have their children's best interests at heart. They do not, however, follow autonomy through to its logical extreme. Rather they practice a style of autonomy within a paradigm which other autonomous educators, myself included, find to be ultimately, if somewhat ironically, limiting.

'Unschooling' without license

Another group who are closely associated with the experience of autonomous education are those who call themselves 'unschoolers'. These form a very significant group of home educators in the United States and increasingly in Britain. They are again highly influenced by John Holt and the organisation and magazine which continues to promote and develop his unschooling theories, *Growing Without Schooling*. Unschooling, as the name suggests, champions a theory of education that is inimical to curricula, timetables and structured learning. It often adopts, instead, an apprenticeship model of learning with children gaining skills, particularly life skills and practical skills by being alongside adults in real life situations. (In this it is not unlike the continuum notion of imitation.) Unschooling demands that children are free to pursue their own interests.

The problem with unschooling, in terms of providing an autonomous education, is not the basic tenet that children can learn without the usual methodology and paraphernalia of schooling, but rather that the term has come to include a very broad spectrum of thought. At one end it makes room for what looks like a liberal schooling approach; not strict subject disciplines, workbooks and timetables, but 'projects' or 'topics', often dovetailing with a child's own interests to a greater or lesser extent, but ultimately imposing an artificial framework on the learning and imposing the boundaries that arise when monitoring and evaluation come into play and education becomes a product to be reflected on. (I will return to this subject more fully in chapters six and seven.)

For example, Wendy Priesnitz writes,

> "*The integrated curriculum unit, which blurs subject distinctions, is a method of organizing learning which uses the principle of integration. Integrated units deal with a topic or theme in its wholeness. During a unit about trees, for example, someone might study real trees, learning how they*

inhabit time, change with the seasons, die and decay (philosophy). They might study the way in which trees sink roots into the soil, drink water, spread their branches, make leaves to catch sunlight, etc. (science). Their learning might also expand to include the other creatures that live alongside trees, such as bugs, birds and larger mammals. Poems or stories and visual art works might be created. Students might share the times they camped in the woods, picknicked under a shady maple, or built a tree house (language arts). They might plant and care for trees. Such an integrated unit on trees does not ignore scientific skills, but integrates them into a multi-dimensional approach. In this way, the study of trees does not merely provide raw material for the learning of concepts and skills. It recognizes that learning about trees involves more than analyzing their structure. It also employs and challenges the other human capacities for sensing, distinguishing, shaping, symbolizing, etcetera.

"Not only does this type of integrated approach allow for recognition of individual learning capacities and styles, it also helps the student develop the qualities and skills necessary to become a responsible, creative and active learner. It allows the parent the flexibility to help the learner capitalize on personal interest and curiosity."

(This article, by Wendy Priesnitz, is reprinted *from Child's Play*, a newsletter formerly published by The Alternate Press and now available at www.life.ca/hs/index.html)

Although this is a liberal and flexible approach to learning, it is not autonomy. The parent has a very definite agenda about what kind of product she wants her child to become. The child's intrinsic motivation to learn is used as a starting point, but then a whole superstructure of so-called related areas are added in, risking killing the original impulse to learn. A child might quite naturally want to paint pictures of trees without doing lessons in botany or natural history or maths with leaves and the delight in painting can soon be lost if these extras are imposed. Autonomous education demands genuine respect of the learner and it is not respectful to grasp at each intimation of an interest as an opportunity for constructing multi-disciplinary topic webs.

On other web pages Priesnitz talks enthusiastically about nurturing self-directed learning, but also adds that an unschooling family can use a mixture of directed and self-directed learning in combinations with which the parents feel comfortable. Similarly Priesnitz speaks against testing, but advises the keeping of subject portfolios, which act as both learning guides and assessment tools. (A subject which I will discuss further in chapter 7.) On the same web-site an article by Jan Hunt extols the virtues of guidance rather than manipulation in learning, but goes on, *"In some circumstances, we should direct learning that is so important we simply cannot leave it to the child"*.

The problem is discovering what are the areas that are so important that the child's autonomy must be compromised? In an interesting survey for the *Taking Children Seriously* journal, David Deutsch examined the proposition that most parents will agree that there are certain vital things which simply have to be taught or insisted upon. But when these vital things are examined there is in fact very little agreement on what they are. Deutsch found that,

> *"... the fact that someone advocates coercion over a given issue would be a very poor predictor of whether that person also advocates coercion over any other issue."*

Moreover he discovered,

> *"... let's consider only the most coercive of the respondents ... There was not a single issue that all of them checked ... Here is a group of people who all advocate coercion over vast swathes of children's lives. Yet there is not a single issue on the list that they all **agree** warrants coercion."*

Unschoolers may be autonomous educators, but they cannot necessarily be assumed so. If the unschoolers who talk about integrated curricula, assessment portfolios or directing learning in so-called important areas do not fit the criteria of supporting intrinsic motivation, then perhaps those who see themselves as libertarian unschoolers do.

Discussing praise and rewards, however, one libertarian unschooler writes,

> *"This is known as external motivation. Some people think there is something wrong with it. I suspect they never realized they had been doing things to please other people until they read Alfie Kohn's 'Punished by Rewards' after which, all of a sudden, they felt their entire lives were shams. The only way to rectify the perceived wrong is to condemn any external motivation as evil - in this case, by slightly twisted logic, the evil of coercion."*

In short, this mother believes that coercion is justified if she feels herself to be first coerced by her children. But this feeling arises for her whenever her children break what she sees as a reasonably and parentally imposed contract between herself and the children which operates like a market contract. She goes on to describe how, from toddlerhood, children must be taught to fend for themselves. This is not as a response to their own explorations or as helpful assistance to their autonomous development, but so that children can quickly learn to meet their contractual obligations to the family and 'pull their own weight'. She goes on,

> *"As a parent you have accepted the obligation to feed, clothe, educate, and house your child until he reaches maturity or until the government considers the child to be an adult. This doesn't mean you have abrogated your rights. Nor does it mean the child can demand food and clothing from you without giving in return."*

These notions that the family can be run along laissez faire capitalist principles of macro economics or that children owe parents contractual obligations are deeply flawed and unlikely to lead to real autonomy. A family is not a company or a scaled model of a nation. Parents and children do not have equal obligations and responsibilities to one another since it is only the parent who decides to bring a child into the world and make a commitment to the child. The child should not have obligations arising from a fact over which they had no choice or control. The libertarian mother quoted above, however, insists,

> *"There are many jobs involved in running a family from earning money to cleaning, cooking, and going on errands. Expecting a fair share from each member of the household isn't unreasonable or coercive. ... Since presumably the children want cooked meals, you can expect meal preparation help from your children. In our case, since our son refuses to learn to use a knife, we've had to make alternative arrangements. Given the choice of dishes or the floors, he picked weekly floor washing. Our chore trade off list is subject to negotiation. In another household - or another year in our's - scrubbing the bathroom or doing the family laundry might seem a suitable trade, ... If he prefers not to, I am prepared not to cook specially for him. Since he has fussy tastes, all that means is I prepare dinner to my husband's tastes or mine. My son won't eat it but will be stuck eating*

crackers for an evening or until he does his share of the work."

This application of markets to family relationships is both brutal and reflects a deep misunderstanding of the unequal obligation that exists between a parent and child. A child who is free only while he is fulfilling the obligations of a bogus contract, which he never agreed to enter into, is not free at all. The weight of extrinsic motivation and coercion is highly likely to lend itself not to autonomous education, but damaged and irrational thinking. The mother concludes,

> *"Some people say this is coercive, but I'm not initiating violence or destructive behavior, nor am I denying him food - he's welcome to learn to use a knife and fix his own food . It is coercive to be obliged to slave after others day after day without getting some return. Besides, it's important that homeschooled children learn to do the chores that make a household run smoothly.*
>
> *"Unschooling libertarian style means allowing your child to study what he wants and when, but it doesn't mean ... you have to live a life of sacrifice. Having one's children happy, useful, productive, and beside you is one of the homeschooling life's greatest rewards."*

It is simply wrong to characterise a child's reluctance to scrub floors in order to earn himself a cooked meal from his mother as the child initiating violence. It rests on the erroneous assumption of a non-existent contract. It also includes the kind of justification of coercion that David Deutsch noted in his survey and which Jan Hunt indicated in her insistence that some things must be taught. In this case the false notion is that chores are so important that they overrule the child's autonomy. Yet this is precisely the kind of thinking which opens the doors to wholesale educational coercion. Perhaps for another parent it is not chores, but maths which is too important not to impose. Those who truly nurture their children's autonomy would agree that self-sacrifice is not the best route for achieving it. Yet they would not agree that what is needed to guard against self sacrifice is the imposition of a binding contract on one's children, but rather a way of living consensually. Autonomous education does not have a product in mind, even when it is such an emotively described product as *"happy, useful and productive"*. Children are not our own art works to be turned out well, but their

own life work to be in continual process. (Quotes taken from the Libertarian Unschooling web-site at:
www.geocities.com/Athens/6529/index1/html)

Not all those who describe themselves as libertarians would want to impose market models on their family or would agree that coercion is justified when children have broken some mythical contract imposed by the parents. The Libertarian Family Network, for example, which is based in Devon, takes a very different line. It stresses the child's right to total respect, to absolute choice over behaviour and expression, to choice in life decisions, to having play recognised as the primary means of learning. Also to having actively involved parents and to learning at home. The Libertarian Family Network lays a great deal of stress on the legacy of damage which parents bring to their parenting, (drawing widely on the work of Alice Miller), and sum up their ideals, *"Each child has the right to be the person they are, to be themselves"*. (*To be Free, A Radical Alternative for Parents and Children*, Issue 1, April 1997. 'Concepts' drawn up by Vidal-Hall family, Harris-Reid family & Lindsay-Turner family.)

In their absolute insistence on meeting the needs of children as they are initially expressed, the Libertarian Family Network may go beyond the ideal of consensual living into a model of adult self-sacrifice. But their concepts and attempts to live with children in new ways do express a very different understanding of libertarianism than is found amongst those who want to impose laissez faire free markets within their own homes.

The advocates of *Taking Children Seriously* are similarly libertarians who do not impose market contracts on family relationships and we will be returning to this branch of autonomous education theory in the next section.

Unschooling can be compatible with autonomous education. When it is, however, merely a more flexible, liberal curriculum masquerading as self-determination, but always within preordained boundaries, then it is not autonomy. When children are being judged against a contract to which they were never signatories, it is not autonomy. When there is, however subtly, a hierarchy of tasks or learning areas that assume more importance than the child, whether the agenda is chores or Shakespeare, it is not autonomy.

Rational thinkers

Characterising children as in some sense natural or mystical unspoilt beings can lead either to neglect or to imposing agendas of what looks 'natural' to parents. Unschooling is of itself not a sufficient guarantor of autonomy. So what theory can autonomous educators rely on in their pursuit of autonomy in their relationships with their children? I would suggest that the most helpful theory of education in its broadest sense is found in the thinking of the proponents of *Taking Children Seriously*. Unlike the educational ideas arising from Liedloff's continuum concept, *TCS* never advocates either a laissez faire approach nor sets up any agenda of how an autonomous child will look and behave. *TCS* does not advocate curricula, no matter how subtly constructed or linked to a child's own interests. It has no concept of any one issue or area of learning that outweighs the child's autonomy. On the other hand, neither does *TCS* advocate self-sacrifice on the part of parents, but instead proposes a consensual style of living based on the idea that given sufficient creativity and rationality all situations can be win-win situations. In short, there exists the possibility of common preferences for any given circumstance.

Taking Children Seriously draws on a range of thinkers in the field of autonomous education, but it does so critically, regarding conjecture and refutation as the fundamental tools of learning. It proposes that children are not examples of humanity unsullied by industrialisation and untainted by modern humanity's evolution away from the romanticised primitive life, but rather that children are ordinary fallible humans who are born with their rationality and creativity intact.

What children lack is not the knowledge of what is best for them in a particular circumstance and not the rational faculties to find solutions, but simply experience. Parents, on the other hand, can offer experience and their own best theories, always with the consciousness that they may be wrong and that what they offer is not the last word. Moreover, parents have a responsibility to children which children do not have to their parents. This moral responsibility ensures that neglectful, laissez faire and disengaged parenting is not an option.

On the *TCS* web-site Sarah Lawrence writes,

> *"It is possible and desirable to bring up children entirely without coercion ... children are entitled to the same rights, respect and control over their lives as adults.*
>
> *"We are critical rationalists, fallibilists and libertarians."*

She goes on,

> *"Educational theory is about the conditions under which human minds do and do not thrive, and about how people learn and how knowledge is created, and about the implications for human creativity, relationships and interactions."*

Closely associated with Popperian philosophy, *TCS* takes what Lawrence describes as, *"a very broad and unified view of what education is."* She writes,

> *"TCS is an educational philosophy. TCS is part of the rationalist tradition, holding that it is possible for human beings, through conjecture, reason and criticism, to come to know (tentatively) and understand truths about the world. TCS is also part of the fallibilist tradition, holding that human beings make mistakes, and that fallibility has important implications for parenting and education. TCS highlights the importance of consent in human relationships, and explains how coercion impairs creativity, which is the ability to think, learn and solve problems in the widest sense. TCS represents a profound criticism of prevailing theories of education and parenting, and provides a positive alternative."*
>
> (Quotes from *TCS* web-site at www.tcs.ac by
> Sarah Lawrence, copyright *TCS*.)

Conclusions: Autonomy, theory and a way forward

Amongst those who adopt what they would describe as an autonomous theory of education, there exists a wide spectrum of thinking. Self-styled autonomous educators are not a homogenous group any more than are conventional educators, but I would suggest that for autonomy to be truly respected certain conditions must be in place.

Firstly, education must be defined very broadly. Education is not just about what schools put onto artificial curricula, but about every aspect of learning, every opportunity for conjecture and refutation. Education is about life and autonomous education is about having the conditions for self-direction within life. Autonomous education does not divide life up into 'education' and 'not education'.

Secondly, autonomous education demands the primacy of intrinsic motivation. It is not the learning style or the content of the learning that is fundamentally at issue. It will probably tend to be the case that autonomous education will look more like a constructivist than a behaviourist model of education and that autonomously educated children will be more likely to be found in informal learning environments, (for example learning through purposive conversation), than in highly structured formal environments, for example. But these remain only broad generalisations and not parameters. What counts above all else is that the activity, whether it be working through a maths CD ROM or watching a soap opera series, arises out of genuine intrinsic motivation.

Thirdly, autonomous education has to free itself from the lure of products and outcomes. There can be no prior agenda of what will result where autonomy is being respected. Writing on the *TCS* list, one poster put it like this,

> *"I now realize that all this time I have been hanging onto the idea that TCS is about creating an environment that will facilitate the 'production' of 'better' children and 'better' potential adults (my own ideas of what 'better' means which has changed somewhat and gotten fairly broad, but has still been there). It has still been to some degree for me about putting that stamp of approval on the child as final 'product', both as a child, and in future adulthood, and on me as a 'good parent'.*

> *"Wow! This has been amazing (and very freeing I might add) to see that this is not only something that I shouldn't have to do and don't have to do, and how deeply disrespectful it is to the child (and to humans in general), but that I can't do anyway even if I think it is my purpose. My children are who they are and will be whatever they will be in the future without my (in)ability to create them in any way. All I can do is get in their way and make life unnecessarily more difficult for them and myself in the process - and thinking of them as a 'product' that will eventually either get or not get a stamp of approval of some sort has been getting in their way, and my way and all our way!*

> *"I can't find the words to say how freeing it is to not be 'responsible' for my children in this way. Instead, I am much*

freer to respond to them. My whole relationship with them seems different - so much more real! This changes everything! It changes how I see the relationship with other people in the world, too. It's amazing. I don't have to meet anybody's stamp of approval either. Including my own. It isn't about stamps of approval and living up to expectations. Amazing!" (*TCS* Internet discussion list, 19.8.99.)

Fourthly, autonomous education assumes that children are rational, creative and innately self determining; that the person who knows what is best in any given situation is the person themselves. Moreover, that all participants in a consensual relationship are capable of changing their preferences to reach an optimum solution for all concerned.

Finally, for autonomous education to operate demands a radical paradigm shift away from conventional thinking in education and parenting. This is a shift in which there are not inevitable losers and winners, but in which all participants are on everyone's side in order to come up with scenarios which best serve the needs of all the individuals involved.

In terms of a developed and continually developing critical theory on which autonomous educators can draw, it is **only taking children seriously**, I believe, which fully meets all of these conditions for genuine autonomy. Many, however, are undoubtedly experimenting with a range of autonomy that can move their children's education only in a positive direction.

Part 2 Introduction:
The experience of autonomous learning

In part one we have seen how a range of educational thinkers support the validity of autonomous education. We have discussed how autonomy can use particular educational theories provided the fundamental requirement of intrinsic motivation is operating. Furthermore, we have surveyed different interpretations of autonomous education, concluding that autonomous education requires an absence of separation between life and learning. Also a stress on intrinsic motivation, a turning away from notions of children as products, an understanding of children as rational, creative and self-determined. And also a major paradigm shift to viewing situations as capable of mutual resolution to the benefit of all parties.

In part two we will look at the practical application of the theory of autonomy in home education. Inevitably, those embarking on autonomous education or those looking in from another perspective raise many questions. Are there basic essentials that all children must learn, by insistence if absolutely necessary? Is autonomous education detrimental to socialisation? If autonomous education demands that coercion be removed from all of family life, what will this mean in practice for the family lifestyle? Given the radical nature of the educational pattern being suggested, how can an autonomously educating parent know for themself or satisfy legal requirements that a full-time, efficient education suitable to the child's age, aptitude and ability is in fact being provided? Are children who have been educated autonomously prepared for the real world in which they must live?

Over the course of the next five chapters I will look at these questions. I shall set out the practical arguments that show that autonomous education is not just a valid theory with a sound moral and philosophical underpinning, but also an eminently practical and rational way to live family life in a new millennium.

Chapter four

The need to know

What about the basics?

Conventional education is fraught with pervasive myths about what are considered to be the essentials of learning, including the acquisition of what are commonly called 'basic skills'. This belief that there is a homogenous body of knowledge which everyone needs to know also gives rise to a rigid stereotyping of what is deemed to be 'age appropriate' learning. There is also a widespread misconception that proper education is something which can be called 'balanced' in education. Autonomous educators do not buy into these misconceptions; 'essentials', 'age stereotyped learning' and 'balance' are all concepts which pose a serious threat to children's intrinsic motivation and their own innate curiosity and drive to learn.

The prevalent thinking of the post-National Curriculum schooling system is that there are certain 'basics' which children need to know. These are often at set ages which seem to be ever younger despite the research and experience of other countries where delayed formal education seems to show no demise in outputs, and often in a prescribed order. Structured education feeds on the fear that without this systematic instruction children will grow up illiterate, innumerate and generally ignorant. On the basis of this unfounded fear, the school system is becoming ever more concerned to maximise its use of structured formal instruction in basic skills. In 1998, for example, David Blunkett, as Secretary of State for Education, launched the literacy hour. This gives children from the age of four or five, (reception class upwards), a highly structured hour of literacy teaching each day plus two further hours of literacy time during the school week. If we assume a forty week school year over the seven years of primary education this amounts to one thousand nine hundred and sixty hours spent on literacy alone. Whereas John Taylor Gatto has estimated that the combined key skills of literacy and numeracy can easily be achieved by a motivated and interested child in up to one hundred hours. The anecdotal evidence of many home educators who follow an autonomous approach confirms that such a basic skill as literacy can be picked up even more quickly than this when the motivation to read is fully intrinsic. In short, children in school are wasting a minimum of one thousand nine hundred and ten of those literacy hours.

Yet this horrendous waste of hours is of less concern than the damage this formal instruction does to children's thinking processes and their ability to motivate and control their own learning. Children are having opportunities for their own intrinsic learning and play closed down to them, not only for the hours spent in 'literacy hour' but by the corresponding amount of damage done to them. They might easily grow up never to take pleasure in a book again.

The reason that literacy is being taught in this way is not because it is essential to be able to read at the age of five or six or seven. After all, in an increasingly technical society the age at which reading is needed to participate in many of society's activities will probably rise. Rather, it is because the logistics of classroom management, with its resulting inability to facilitate that intrinsic learning of individuals, demand such wasteful systems in order for the system to survive, as one mother pointed out,

> *"My point (is) that the age set for literacy is to enable the system to work, teachers need children to be able to read. Home educated children are able to learn without being able to read and can therefore learn to read when it is best for them."*

Home educating parents whose children learn by an autonomous route know that their children will acquire the skills they need to take advantage of their environment and pursue their own aspirations. One home educating parent puts it like this,

> *"I suppose I agree that, to get along in our society, there are certain 'essentials'. However I am convinced that a child can easily recognise that, even before they can speak, and that children have a natural desire to learn those 'essentials' so that they can make sense of their world. I don't agree with force feeding schemes of maths, English and science."*

The list of what constitutes 'essentials' will, of course, vary across context, and, in an environment of autonomous education, the list will rest on what the child defines as essential, as one parent sums up,

> *"I think the essentials that need to be taught are the things our children want us to teach them or what they want to learn on their own. These things may not include multiplication and division operations (which can be done by calculator anyway), but answers to questions that have meaning to the child."*

What autonomously home educating parents across the spectrum agree on is that however the 'essentials' are defined they will be acquired without resort to lesson plans, set hours or externally imposed motivation, but rather,

> *"The truth is a child will learn whatever he or she determines important. Walking and talking are two of the most difficult 'essentials' a person ever learns, but, even as infants, we observed and determined that we would learn these things, and continued in our own individual ways until we did. No parents, no teachers, no 'You have to learn this for your own good' lectures. Just ourselves and our innate ability of self-determination. It's as if parents don't recognise that we did that, because after we learn these very important things almost everything in our lives, including learning, is determined by parents, teachers, etc. and all without any input from the young person. Is it any wonder that so many students at university level have no idea what they want to do with their lives, now that they have finally been given the right to choose."*

Another autonomously educating parent points out that with regard to the 'Three Rs',

> *"I maintain that a child in modern Western society would have to be kept in a cupboard in order not to learn these things. Left to themselves, children will automatically learn the things that they need to function in the society in which they live. On the other hand, children who are subjected to 'teaching' may decide not to learn those things because they cannot keep up with some arbitrary idea of the standard they should have reached and it is less damaging to their self-esteem to exercise control and refuse to learn."*

This confidence that such skills as reading will be learnt by any child who is in a literate environment is widely shared and experienced by parents of children for whom autonomy is central to their education. The parent continues:

> *"If by essentials (one means) reading, then I don't think, it needs to be taught although I do think it will be learned along the way. Both my children had books around from an early age, were read to and encouraged, e.g. by visits to the library. One read easily at an early age (a confidence booster for the no school, no schemes approach) and then the second one took four years longer... However now, in their teens, they both read all the time."*

Autonomously educating parents are culturally peculiar in respecting their children's intrinsic learning capability, and in trusting that children will use this capability at the right time and in the right spheres for their best educational growth. They are also, however, acutely aware that not to respect their children in such ways can have devastating consequences for the learning process. This is how one home educating father explains,

> *"It's easy to imagine that speech is naturally acquired, and be sufficiently relaxed about that not to leap in and muck it up, but reading and writing seem such relatively recent cultural artefacts in the development of our species that it is easy to think that maybe, these skills can't be allowed to develop in the same way, and we really do have to teach these otherwise they won't be acquired.*

> *"This is not the case. Exactly the same amazingly subtle and natural processes can be relied on here as well. I didn't know this until fairly recently. The education system gets to most children before they are allowed to invent and continuously re-invent their own spelling, so you never get to see this. We don't have to understand 'how' it works, it is sufficient that it does. What we do need to understand are the conditions under which it will best thrive, and the first principle is non-interference. After that, comes an environment where books are a source of pleasure, and read to children when they want them. A rich environment is pretty hard to avoid these days in any case. As John Holt has argued (in* Growing Without Schooling*) a child has as much chance of not acquiring literacy as they have of turning into a crocodile.*

> *"But there is an efficient method of keeping a child from literacy. Take one damaged human being loaded to the gills with anxiety about children failing to learn literacy unless*

taught, someone who knows less than nothing about natural learning processes, call them a teacher, put them in a place of absolute power over your child, then force that child to learn the bizarre nonsense methodology in that teacher's head which has no point of reference in the head of any child whatsoever, and moreover force this garbage on them at an inappropriate stage of their physical and mental development. That will do the job!"

Autonomous educators are confident that children will learn whatever children deem for themselves to be essential, whether it is the required body of knowledge to enter a medical career or the history of twentieth century film-making or how to build a tree house. In educational law there is no concept of attempting to cause a child to know any particular essentials, but rather of ensuring that education is 'efficient'. (See Appendix 1 for a full discussion of the legal guidelines with regard to home education.)   What could be more efficient than a child learning something to suit his or her own intrinsic and individual purposes?

In 1981 the judgement in the Harrison case, (as can be seen in the Guidelines contained in Appendix 1), defined efficient as *"that which it sets out to achieve"*. Autonomous education sets out not to transmit a body of essentials which can be systematically worked through and ticked off the curriculum list. Autonomous education sets out to support children in achieving what they wish to achieve and negotiating their own creative and individual place in the world according to their own intrinsic motivation. It achieves that which it sets out to do for as long as children remain the prime movers in their own learning.

The school system assumes that learning is a process that requires a specific methodology and that formal teaching is the primary method for imparting large amounts of knowledge as quickly as possible. In reality, however, it is information rather than real knowledge that is passed on and even then it is questionable how truly fixed this information becomes in the recipient's mind. It is not essential that children should be coerced into learning specific things in order to give them the chance to enter academic disciplines at a later stage. Rather, passionate interest is what can be relied upon to galvanise the ability to pick up large amounts of information or knowledge to areas that become appealing.

Learning by age?

Age stereotyping of learning goes hand in hand with the culture of 'essential knowledge'. The school system clearly defines reading ages and the national curriculum sets up age-related attainment targets in what are considered to be the core subjects of English, maths and science. Whilst it is true that education law speaks of education needing to be 'suitable to his age' it does not elucidate on what constitutes suitability. Home educators are not bound by the national curriculum or by school-defined measurements. So it is a mistake to jump from the true belief that education has to be suitable to a child's age, to the mistaken conclusion that there is any consensus on exactly what that means and how it might be judged. Whilst British state education is moving towards formal teaching and defined attainment targets at younger ages, many other countries, even in their formal education, do not introduce such 'subjects' as literacy until the age of seven, believing it to be educationally detrimental to begin earlier. Alternative theories of education, (for example the Steiner model), similarly actively discourage young reading as detracting from other abilities.

Autonomous educators are in the advantageous position of providing education which is suitable to a child's age, not on the grounds of a theory which insists on letter recognition at age four, or another theory which says children should not be allowed to be literate at age six. But rather on the grounds that the individual child is able to determine, with the provision of a rich supply of information and support, those things which aid that particular child's learning at that particular age. All children aged six are not a homogenous group. Obviously schools treat them as such, either from a management or an ideological position, or a combination of the two. But the truth is that autonomous education prizes individual creativity and learning and cannot therefore acquiesce in mechanical age markers as an indication of learning. This is not to say that age is totally irrelevant, but its relevance will be open to a broad degree of individual variance from one child to another.

It might, for example, be age appropriate for child A to be reading fluently at the age of three, whilst it is just as appropriate for child B to not read text at the age of ten. One home educating father has noted,

> *"Our 10 year-old still remains largely unbothered about his literacy skills, although in his own way, he is still acquiring these skills all the time, he just can't read a book yet...*

"He does however learn a great deal, and often corrects me on matters of fact when we are in conversation, and it turns out that he knows more about something I'm trying to explain to him than I do. I'm sure that if these relatively modern media (TV and computer) were not available to him, he would probably be reading proficiently by now in the absence of other stimulating and attractive sources of information.

"I'm also sure that as he continues to come up against the natural limitations of these media, and finds that more of what he wants is in books, this will provide its own incentive, and may, as others have discovered before us, all come quite quickly."

Another father of an autonomously educated child wrote,

"From Chambers dictionary...
Illiterate: unacquainted with literature: Without book learning: Uneducated: Ignorant: Unable to read

"Our non reading 10 year-old could never be considered ignorant. I would like to think that he could never be considered uneducated. He has books from which he learns and is, thanks to the Walkman and audio books on tape, acquainted with far more literature than me (despite my many years of 'efficient' education) and, I suspect, many other 10 year-olds. He would be found to be imaginative, creative, articulate and computer literate. He has never found a need to learn to read. I, for one, would like to think that we could show that, with all those pluses against one small minus, he was enjoying a full and efficient education and was a child preparing for life in modern civilised society."

Another unwelcome feature of age stereotyping is that it concentrates on traditional academic disciplines rather than on the whole range of learning possibilities open to autonomously educated children. Thus a ten-year-old child whose learning is self-motivated might, (quite appropriately), not have acquired the reading skills to which a school would aspire. The same child, however, may very well be able to design and construct a complex model using carpentry skills or electronics skills. Or the child may have a deep knowledge of astronomy or natural history, or have developed animation or drama skills, or have any number of other interests that would not immediately spring to mind when looking at age appropriate learning from a conventional educational perspective.

Is it balanced?

Hand in hand with this enormous and misguided concern that the 'basics' must be drummed into children by certain ages, and by whatever intensive means happen to be the educational flavour of the day, there often goes the dogmatic and unfounded assumption that for education to be 'proper' it must be 'balanced'. What is meant by 'balanced' is not something that can be defined by any objective educational standard, but is rather a highly coloured and often emotive term emanating from the current agenda of mainstream schooling trends.

There is nowhere in educational law any requirement for imparting a given list of knowledge or information and no requirement that education should be about 'balance'. Yet time and again home educating parents who have dealings with local education authorities report being criticised both for insufficient attention to the magical 'essentials' and for 'failing' to enforce an educational style which is 'balanced' according to the fluctuating definition being implemented in schools. Thus a family who follow the national curriculum at home were recently criticised by their LEA for not having instituted the 'Literacy Hour'! Another family, whose children were producing projects of a far higher 'reading age' than would have been expected in school, were told they needed more practical work, whilst another family was advised to attend to its gap in the provision of team sports.

If such criticisms are levelled at families who are following some structured and parent-led agenda of home education, then it is easy to see that children pursuing their own interests on an autonomous basis are hardly likely to be perceived as falling into the category of receiving a 'balanced' education. Real education, however, is not about balance. There is no magic list of ingredients which must be combined and imbibed in some set order to produce an educated person, as autonomously home educating parents recognise,

> *"Better still if the child can manage to tailor their own particular 'program' of study by following their own interests. Are we not, as home educating parents, facilitators rather than teachers, making it our job to understand our own children better than anybody and ensuring that we allow access to learning opportunities appropriate to our children? In my opinion what suffers most when children are presented with material at an inappropriate level FOR THEM is their*

*self-esteem. Lack of self-esteem, coupled with lack of interest
is bound to lead to failure."*

Educational law talks about suitability to age, ability and aptitude,
but not about this spurious notion of balance. Yet too often those
educating autonomously are undermined by the pervasiveness of a
system that does not trust either children or parents and which is so
impatient for outcomes that process is lost. Responding to this
pressure one father wrote,

> *"Maybe these parents (autonomous educators) have their
> sights and hopes set on a level of competence, pleasure, and
> interest in literacy in their growing child beyond what they
> themselves were allowed to attain, and stand back sometimes
> nervously, waiting what can seem like interminable ages for
> something to fall into place and vindicate that shaky faith in
> the possibility of something better than we were allowed, but
> with a hostile and uncomprehending world bristling with
> inspectors, hovering around us menacingly, waiting for us to
> fail and vindicate the perpetuation of their prison system."*

The criteria of essentials and balance are in fact artificial constructs
which owe more to the institutionalisation of education than to any
of the intrinsic needs of children in the constant process of learning.
But so often they have become ingrained into our curriculum
conditioned mentalities in such a way that many have ceased to ask
why a certain thing should be learned at a certain age or even at all,
depending on the needs of the individual child. Yet, rationally, we
know that it is not the case that the self-aware or successful or
creative adults we know are those who learned a particular thing
only at a particular age or who had an education that contained just
the right mix of balanced subjects. Indeed, as Pamela Kerr noted in
an article in the *TCS* journal, issue 22,

> *"By expecting everyone to be well rounded, we may well be
> blunting genius by taking time away from the development of
> one, particular skill."*

As home educators who take seriously the need for autonomy in
educational development, we need to be very wary of any argument
which suggests that there are certain things that must be learned or
that some artificially defined breadth of academic subjects
constitutes what children need to know. If we are serious that
autonomy is essential to true learning then we must be prepared to
take seriously the need to facilitate and nurture our children's

interests as the only essentials to their growth of knowledge. This is even when these interests fall completely outside the normal prescriptive categories of what constitutes 'education'. As Sarah Lawrence has remarked in *TCS* journal, issue 24,

> *"All the wonderful things parents say about interest-led education mean very little unless they actually do help their children to follow their interests wherever they lead. If the children are going to run into a wall of parental intransigence every time their interests take them over the artificial 'Education' line, their learning will be curtailed and their intellectual development will be sabotaged at every turn."*

Education which is genuinely autonomous, child-led, and in no way coerced, requires that the parents facilitate whatever the child's sphere of interest happens to be, whether it is nuclear physics or watching a series of television soap operas, (a theme which will be expanded on in chapter five). The notion of balance is not pertinent to intrinsically motivated education and the concept of what constitutes essential learning can be only what the child, assisted by parents who ensure a stimulating, choice-rich environment, determines and defines in a continual process of growth.

Will they learn nothing?

Behind these notions of an essential list to be learned by certain ages and according to some predefined agenda of balance, there lurks the fear that without structured, transmissive teaching children will learn nothing. This is a false understanding both of learning and of the nature of children. The whole question of what is essential to education and the location of balance in education is, for the autonomous educator, not a question of subjects, disciplines, timetable or age appropriate topics, but rather one of ethos.

In researching this book, I asked parents to think about those things that are helpful to the education process and those which are harmful. The answers did not include anything about literacy by age seven or the so-called 'need' for knowledge of multiplication tables. But rather they concentrated exclusively on the conditions for learning to take place within an individual without harm being done.

Examples of what parents had come to see as essential to helping the learning process were:

- the child's desire to know or to acquire a skill

- a way of getting access to the knowledge
- an encouraging adult or another child already competent in that skill
- the ability to say when they want to change activities or to carry on all day if they wish
- confidence to ask questions in public, use phone, quiz museum attendant, etc.
- freedom to experiment without fear of failure and negative criticism
- loving (our children) and expressing that love without regard to what one assumes they are or are not learning
- providing an environment or access to an environment where exposure to a variety of interests, people, beliefs and relationships is possible
- lots of verbal interaction
- trusting the child
- allowing the children to develop at their own pace
- having space to think their own thoughts
- having people around who are interested and interesting, but not interested in making you do things.

On the other hand, there was also a very clear list of what harms the learning process and destroys true education, much of which would be seen as 'essential' to conventional educators:

- being expected to have overwhelming desires to learn Physics because its 10 am on Tuesday and English because its 10.30!
- learning things to please someone else or to forget after the test
- learning by rote but not understanding
- an adult/helper who dominates or does not take an interest
- having Mum or Dad deal with all the adults in your life
- humiliation, negative criticism
- connecting our love of our children to what and when they learn
- limiting the child or young person's exposure to only family or school determined interests, people, beliefs and relationships
- not taking an active interest in their learning processes, being too busy to interact with the child, offering no help or strategies
- all adult imposed agendas of what to learn, when to learn it, and how to learn it.
- testing.

Intellectual development, for those who support autonomous education, is not and never can be a tick box process by which children move through a preordained curriculum acquiring the correct gobbits of information or skill at the correct time only to be so soon forgotten again. Intellectual development is an unpredictable adventure for individuals whose creativity, flexibility and intrinsic motivation is valued and nurtured. When this ethos is achieved, autonomous home educators can relate a multitude of examples of how intrinsic motivation and intrinsic curiosity lead to continual learning. Parents, who have themselves often learned in highly structured and creativity-limiting environments, report an enormous range of interests and developing competencies amongst autonomously learning children in a multitude of arenas. Many of them are entirely or partly closed to their peers who are coerced into schools.

What is more, these competencies are developed without the stress of forcing and cajoling and pressurising unwilling children to fulfil parental or governmental agendas. Consider the intrinsic goal is to be learning to swim, rock climbing, computer programming, new leaps forward in maths, a thorough acquaintance with every detail of every Star Trek script, advanced photography, bird watching or cooking the perfect pancake. Then the parental role of suggesting, modelling, stimulating, providing access to materials or the optimum environment always remains in the supportive sphere, and there is the constant satisfaction for the learner that he or she owns his or her own learning.

It is simply not possible for a child to be in such a supportive environment and 'learn nothing'. The question is actually merely a betrayal of the assumption that only certain things count as educational, only certain things should be valued as activities, interests and skills and only certain narrowly prescribed topics are essential, appropriate and balanced. This is simply not the case.

Chapter five

Autonomy and socialisation

All home educating parents face questions about how their children will find social outlets and become social creatures, but such questions are particularly acute for autonomously educating families. There is a misconception that children who are not 'forced' to learn in a particular way will have corresponding difficulties in socialising or even in becoming socially responsible members of society. There is an impression that such children are more likely to be selfish, demanding and closed to input or that they will suffer from a lack of independence. Such impressions are mistaken. They rely on a poor understanding of the educational importance of being at the centre of one's own world and having one's childhood needs met. They mistake autonomy for neglect or permissiveness and totally fail to deal with the opportunities which autonomous education affords for creative criticism and the continual reappraisal of one's own theories.

Autonomously educated children are not a blanket group with a blanket character. Like other groups of children, they number amongst themselves those who are extrovert and those who are more introverted. Being in control of their social relations, however, frees autonomously educated children from the burdens of having to mix only with a preordained and artificial group in which a wide variety of stressful and coercive pressures can dominate and damage their lives.

Will they mix?

It is the general experience of parents whose children take the lead in their own education that socialisation becomes a broader and more fulfilling experience than can generally be achieved in schools where most children have no choice over attending. One mother says,

> "I think most home educated children are used to being treated as people rather than one in a group of children and relate well to others of all ages."

Another confirms,

> *"I have found autonomous education greatly enhances a child's ability to socialise and negotiate with people outside of the immediate family. This is primarily because the child has a strong self-confidence and self-respect gained via his or her experience with thinking for themselves and making their own determinations."*

The combination of autonomy and being in the real world rather than a constructed world of same age peers has an enormously positive influence on the socialisation process, as has been summed up by one home educating parent,

> *"Instead of spending so much of their lives having no need to socialise or negotiate (as in school), they are spending their time within the community that they have to negotiate as an adult. In school the relationships with others are contrived. They can learn from the adults around them if they spend time as equals with them."*

Another parent concludes,

> *"Our children are sociable, assertive and confident. Free from the competitiveness and inevitable difficulties of achieving externally imposed agendas, they do not learn fear or inferiority."*

It is certainly true that home educated children and most especially those following an autonomous route do not receive the same kind of socialisation as their schooled peers. There is no doubt that this is perceived as a threat by some more conventional educators and thinkers. It is a perennial complaint against home educated children that they fail to receive the correct dosage of socialisation; a not infrequent claim from local educational authorities and their support services. Other minds, however, have questioned not only whether school type socialisation is something to be sought after or emulated, but also whether such school type socialisation is compatible with true education and the growth of knowledge.

Socialisation and homogeneity

Thomas Szasz, arguing against the use of mental health workers in the school socialisation process, has put forward the view that real education and socialisation, (of the type found in schools), are, at least partly if not wholly, antagonistic processes,

> *"Personality development is a complex biological, cultural, social, and personal affair. The kind of personality an*

individual develops depends partly on the kinds of values his family and his society cherish and despise - by word as well as by deed. The kind of personality modern Western man has grown to value in the last few centuries is embodied in the religions, laws, morals, and customs of this civilization: it is a person adequately socialized but possessing an authentic individuality. However, the precise proportion of the two ingredients necessary for a suitable balance is variously defined, and, regardless of the proportion, the achievement of such a balance is an exceedingly delicate task. This is why the concept of a 'normal man' - or, more generally, of life as a well-executed dramatic production - is so elusive."

Szasz notes that unlike socialisation,

"the broader aim of education is not so much socially correct performance as creative innovation, with its own, fresh standards of value."

For Szasz, whilst school socialisation looks for homogeneity education should nurture not only diversity, but subversion in the sense of discovering seemingly radical new ideas as a means of constantly improving the social order. Szasz goes on,

"This aim (of socialisation) is best achieved by discouraging idiosyncratic behavior and exploration, and by encouraging conduct favoring group solidarity. Thus, the reduction of choice and alternatives, though inimical to critical education, is essential to socialization, especially in a mass society."

Again he argues,

"In the end, the aim of critical teaching can only be to provide conditions favorable for the development of the autonomous personality, whereas the aim of socialization can only be the opposite - to provide the conditions favorable for the development of the heteronomous personality."

In an autonomous learning situation the delicate and complicated balance between being a social creature and the growth of personal knowledge are not put under the enormous and artificial pressures for conformity and homogeneity which exist in schools or, to a lesser extent, in structured home learning environments. Rather, children in these environments can be supported in negotiating their own solutions to complex social situations without the necessity of having to surrender their integrity or sense of self.

(Thomas S. Szasz, 'Mental Health Services in the Schools', from the collection of essays, 'Ideology and Insanity' Doubleday Anchor, 1970, pp. 140-144)

For autonomously educated children socialisation is not about imbibing a monolithic body of (often arbitrary) rules for conduct, many of which have no other agenda than control, submission to authority and adherence to a pecking order. Rather, it is about establishing which social outlets maximise their own creativity, learning and chosen contributions to the social order in the most pleasant and fulfilling ways.

The theory that autonomously home-educated children are more likely to be socially incompetent is one based on prejudice or on untested and entrenched assumptions. There is still a commonly held notion that children must learn to 'socialise' in large groups within even larger institutions in order to fit them for society. This is largely based on a failure to question why schools are organised in this way. School organisation reflects a societal organisation that was more prevalent at the Industrial Revolution, fitting children for conformity in factory work and other large scale organisations, but whilst schools have largely maintained this once 'appropriate' structure, society has moved on.

> "Post industrial society is characterised by much smaller units of production... Concepts such as self-management, teams and home working become common...

> "Individuals are no longer tied to belief systems regulated by an homogeneity of life experience. ...

> "The education system reflects industrial culture. The education debate of the mid nineteenth century centred on keeping young people off the streets, freeing their parents to work in factories and preventing them from falling into immoral practices. The very structure of schools reflected life in a factory: large classes, a rigorous code of discipline and strict hierarchical structure. School was a microcosm of society and a foretaste of the future for its alumna."

(Fortune-Wood, M., *Education Otherwise*, national newsletter no.115, April 97)

Not only is such an artificial form of socialisation totally inimical to the concept of autonomy, but it is simply no longer the case that it can in any sense be seen as appropriate for society in general. This does not, however, mean that home-educated children need be in any sense socially isolated. Rather, it means that children are able to choose their groups according to their own needs and personalities. After all, it must be remembered that socialisation is not a numbers game; a great deal of social isolation can exist in the school playground in the midst of the crowd.

For home-educated children, particularly those who enjoy autonomy of education, social situations are not limited to age or other artificial peer groups or to specific and regulated times of the day. Instead, these children are freed, like adults, to find peers based on common interests or mutual attraction. Neither does this need to become a separatist endeavour, which marginalises children or confines them to a rarefied group. Home-educated children exist not in an institution, but in the real world. They learn to negotiate the social situations of clubs, interest groups, shops, streets, other homes, etcetera, in the world at large and have enlarged opportunities for socialising on the same basis as adults. Moreover, they can avail themselves of these opportunities at their own pace and in their own way, allowing confidence and self-esteem to be a natural part of socialising. This runs contrary to fears that autonomously home-educated children are likely to be morbidly dependent on their parents and unable to function without constant parental protection and, ironically, can occur by virtue of there being no inflexible age requirement as to when children 'must' develop independence.

Missing out?

There is a commonly held assumption that by not going to school, children are missing out on some valuable aspect of socialisation that only school can provide. It is a wrong assumption, and one which Roland Meighan, amongst others, has questioned effectively. Like the belief that children must learn maths or Shakespeare, Meighan calls the belief in the need for school-based socialisation a superstition.

Meighan notes that in his own educational experiment, the school at Beacon Hill, Bertrand Russell later admitted that,

> "... he seriously overestimated the amount of time children need in the company of each other. 15,000 hours is a long time to be forced to spend in the company of a selected number of your peers..."

Turning to recent newspaper reports, Meighan draws attention to the prevalence of bullying in schools,

"Children now expect bullying to be a regular feature of school life. A national survey commissioned by Family Circle magazine showed that eight out of 10 have suffered at least one sustained attack. On average, the first bullying experience can now be expected at the age of eight."

Meighan goes on to point out the rising incidences of weapon carrying, substance abuse problems, even in primary schools, and general negative peer pressure. Commenting on recent initiatives to lower truancy rates, supposedly to lower social exclusion, Meighan asks,

"'Exclusion from what?' you might be tempted to ask. 'Weapons, or drugs, or bullying?'

"... Home-schooling families actually create a much higher quality of social life in their practice of family-centred education, in three ways. First of all they use the home as a springboard into the community using libraries, museums, places of interest in both town and country. In the process they rub shoulders with people of all ages. ... Secondly, they locate and join groups such as Scouts, Guides, and Woodcraft Folk, as well as groups or classes in judo, swimming and other sports, or natural history and other pursuits . Thirdly, they seek out other home-schooling families and do things in co-operation."

(Quotes taken from *'A superstition called socialisation'*, from *Educational Heretics* web-site. A version of this appeared in the Roland Meighan column of *Natural Parent* magazine, Nov/Dec 1998.)

The social self?

It is true that autonomously educated children are not robbed of the notions that they are the centre of their own universe and neither are they disabused of the notion that only they can finally determine what is in their best interests. Autonomously home-educated children are confident that their sense of self is not a 'sin', but the basis for learning. Having a strong sense of self is not in any way inimical to developing a sense of social responsibility and thought for others.

Autonomously educated children are not monsters in the making. A parent who respects his or her child's autonomy is not one who believes that she/he should never share their own moral opinions and indeed a wide range of moral opinions with the child. Whilst final decisions rest with the individual, even a very young individual, parents are an invaluable source of experience, opinion, example and creative criticism.   Respect of autonomy bears no relation to neglect or to any form of laissez faire parenting, which abandons children, without critical and respectful input, into a moral vacuum or to whatever other influences happen by to fill up the gap. Thus one parent writes,

"I feel very strongly that it is how children see others relating to each other that influences how they relate. I don't see autonomous education as precluding setting my children a good example of respect and caring for other people."

Whilst another adds,

"I would say that neglect leads to children who are selfish, demanding, unco-operative, etc. Autonomy should be supported by adults who lovingly assist the child to see the point of view of other people and to make decisions that take other points of view into account."

Writing on the TCS web-site Sarah Lawrence says,

"When someone complains of a child being, or growing up to be 'self-centred'... what they are really saying is, 'He is doing what he thinks right and I fear what he may think.'
... There is a terrible fear abroad, the fear that if we think too clearly about issues of right and wrong, we shall tend to choose wrong, so that the only hope of salvation is the suppression of independent thought."
(Quoted from www.tcs.ac by Sarah Lawrence, copyright TCS)

One parent notes,

"Autonomy in education, as with the other areas of living, provides the experience of taking responsibility for attaining what is desired, including learning ...   negative traits seem more often to be exhibited in kids within forced learning environments ...   who are tired of being coerced or forced, and thus are rebelling in any way they can."

Another mother expresses her satisfaction with her children's sense of social caring like this,

"I think this comes from a misunderstanding of what autonomy means. Many people seem to think that it means learning 'nothing'. They have an image of a wild child, who

runs in the field all day, every day, who has no curiosity to learn and never develops beyond the stage they were allowed to 'run wild'.

"I think it stems from the fact that we have only known life in this century and therefore have grown up to think that learning means schooling and that without it we would all be uneducated and 'backward'. It is hard for people to think of a time when we didn't have schooling, yet we still had intelligent, co-operative, socially adjusted adults...

"In practice I think the opposite happens to what people imagine, in that given the respect of being allowed autonomy and assumed worthy of it, children learn to use the same kind of respect toward others. Given subservience, that is what they will learn to use toward others younger than themselves, or later in life, in 'lower' hierarchical positions."

One father says quite simply,

"'Selfish, demanding and uncooperative' are products of frustration, neglect, and unmet need, not of being free individual, valued and engaged with."

Underlying many of the views that 'allowing' autonomy will contribute only to social irresponsibility and callousness is a plethora of populist concepts that often come under the umbrella of 'spoiling'. Conventional parenting wisdom cautions that children who do not experience resistance to their desires will be just those individuals who become oblivious to the needs and humanity of others. Not only is this contradicted by anecdotal evidence such as that cited above, but it is also very poor theory. I have already noted the opposing paradigm proposed by Alice Miller that it is unmet needs which are likely to cause overwhelming urges for antisocial control of others. Furthermore, it is quite feasible to assert that this false polarisation of meeting one's own needs and being sensible of the needs of others is not only unnecessary, but positively harmful to children's thinking. It is simplistic to assume that children must choose between themselves and others. The choice is rather always one of deciding upon the right course of action. This is not something that can be decided upon by appeal to mechanical rules. Rather, it is a process which demands the kind of creative and rational thinking that arises out of having had one's own autonomy respected and nurtured. It is, of course, not only possible, but essential that in respecting autonomy parents do not fall into the neglectful trap of never sharing their own strong moral opinions with children or never offering criticism of behaviour and attitudes which they believe to be wrong. If these moral beliefs and criticism have the force of rationality and are offered without coercion then it is highly likely that confident, rational, autonomous children will be able to weigh the arguments without fear of rejection.

Of course, it needs to be added that how autonomously educated children are perceived as social beings will depend, in some measure, on the prejudices about children by which they are being judged. Autonomously educated children are likely to join in with adult conversation, to expect to be paid equal attention when they speak and to want information on which they can make informed decisions rather than simply being told what to do. As one autonomous educator remarks,

> *"People may see them (children) as demanding if they think children's natural role is to be submissive."*

Submission, unquestioning obedience to authority, silence in the presence of adults, are as inimical to an autonomous child as is complete disregard for others. Neither of these positions is likely to aid true learning and growth, which is after all the aim of autonomous education.

Self-directed socialisation

Autonomous home education is about self-direction. A child who wants a lot of social engagement should be helped to find just that. A child who prefers his or her own company should be equally respected. Much of what passes for socialisation in schools is either about becoming functional and docile according to someone else's standards or about fitting in to a milieu that might well feel alien and even hostile. Children do not need such artificial and often painful socialisation. Neither do children need to be moulded and coerced in order to learn to make right and social decisions. Socialisation is often the first problem that people raise with any form of home education. At a recent conference of clergy men and women, one of my colleagues asked how I overcome the socialisation 'problem'. I smiled and said, *"Well actually with great difficulty. It takes a lot of creativity to handle all the requirements of such a hectic social life, but we seem to manage."*

Chapter six

Education as life

Eradicating the lines of demarcation

Autonomous education is not only about the narrow field of experience that is conventionally slotted into the boundaries of schooling. If autonomy of education is advocated and respected then it must necessarily encompass the total family lifestyle and preclude all other forms of coercion. The role of play, attitudes to television and other media, arbitrary rules about such things as bedtime, food, dress code, use of time and so on all come into play. To limit any aspect of autonomy is fundamentally to affect the integrity of the autonomy.

Education in school has clearly defined parameters, even if its tentacles are ever extending under the guise of homework, it remains a defined body of thinking with a clear core, (the 'basics' of literacy and numeracy). David Blunkett, as Minister for Education, has been heard to say that if children are not in school they are not learning. This is clearly false. For those pursuing an autonomous education at home, the boundaries between life and education are much less distinct and much less artificial. Autonomous education is not only a valid theory of education, but also an embracing lifestyle. The way in which autonomously educating parents interact with their children often takes on a whole new tenor in which non-coercion becomes part of the total educational theory and package.

I have already indicated that education which is genuinely autonomous, child-led and in no way coerced, requires that the parents facilitate whatever the child's sphere of interest happens to be. We have also seen, (both in the list of essential requisites for autonomous education provided by parents, and in the conclusions of chapter three above), that there is a fundamental stress on the primacy of intrinsic motivation. This requires that parents let go of preconceived and often irrational views of what counts as 'education' and cease from defining when learning has taken place inside another person's mind (their child's).

In order to value education truly and to foster autonomy in education there must be no artificial definitions of what is educational. Unfortunately this is a point on which much unschooling theory breaks down. As Sarah Lawrence pointed out · in her article, *Taking Education Seriously* (TCS 24), many unschoolers will gladly let their children off chores or stay up late if they are reading a book or working out a maths problem, but will demand that the dishes be washed or the lights turned out if they are 'merely' watching a TV programme or playing a computer game. She rightly points out,

> *"... since they can escape bedtime, chores and other unpleasant things by reading, **they are being pressurised to read**."*

Lawrence goes on,

> *"They are switching off the very engine that they are relying on to power their children's education, namely the children's intrinsic motivations ... It follows that freedom in the matter of academic study is inseparable from freedom in the matter of chores, bedtime and anything else."*

The logic is simple and compelling. As soon as we begin to construct a hierarchical value system in which reading a book is more approved of than watching a soap opera, or doing a maths problem is more worthy than lying an the sofa gazing into space, then we are interfering with autonomy. We are making judgements about the possible learning taking place in someone else's mind and we are damaging the process of intrinsic motivation which is at the core of autonomous education.

Autonomous education goes far beyond questioning the boundaries between subject disciplines or accepted academic compartments. Autonomous education embraces all learning. It cannot be kept pigeon-holed in one section of life. This certainly seems to be the consensus of parents, who are attempting to educate autonomously,

> *"I cannot, in my own experience, separate home education from autonomous education and autonomous living. Everything that we do is part of education (e.g. we may watch a TV show that is not officially 'educational' that sparks off a number of other activities)."*

Not only do education demarcation lines cease to have effect, but the whole family ethos changes with autonomous education,

> *"When authentic autonomous education is involved the family's lifestyle would become very flexible and would require a high level of real communication between its members. This would manifest a family, which would truly be a home for the learner, a place or people he returns to no matter how far his journeys take him. This would be an authentic family, not the Disney cartoon vision of family so many people try to emulate."*

Another parent puts it like this,

> *"... rather than separating children's lives from the adult's lives ... our children come out with us to restaurants, parties, meetings, work, the bank, solicitor, estate agent, etc. This means that they know what is going on in the family life and are involved in decisions that many families keep away from the children."*

Erasing the lines of demarcation between 'education' and 'not education' is a far-reaching and radical step. Those that take this step find themselves with a model of consensual living which conventional educational theory would not even recognise as belonging to the language of education. For autonomous educators, however, it is the only moral standpoint from which to foster an education that does not damage children in terms of how they think. This being the case, the arena for learning is enormously expanded and the opportunities for damaging the learning process decrease only as coercion is eliminated from all areas of life.

The role of coercion

Of course all of this assumes that coercion is an impediment to learning and autonomous educators need to offer some justification for this belief. There are those who would argue that coercion, (often more subtly packaged as encouragement, guidance, manipulation or insistence), is necessary in order to ensure that children learn. They do so either because they have a set of unexamined assumptions about what must be learned through external motivation, or because they believe that the child will not understand the reasons for learning certain essential things. We have already seen that there is no consensus of any magic list of what must be learned by a child. Even if we could agree what such a list might look like, it is highly unlikely that a non-coerced child would not acquire the basic skills to survive in any given culture. A belief that certain things are necessary for a full and creative life does not lead to a justification of coercion. It rather provides the motive force for parents to share their best theories with children, who can trust that they still retain the control over their own thinking, and who will therefore be most likely to happily adopt theories which seem to them compelling on their own merits. If a parent cannot rationally convince a child that x is good in itself, then the child might very well be right to reject x.

The belief that parents must decide for their children what to learn because their children will not understand this for themselves is equally flawed. Children are obviously at a disadvantage in terms of having less experience and therefore might not consider certain things. What is required, therefore, are sensitive and engaged parents who can use their experience to point out possible sources of learning; parents who can offer constructive criticism and reasoned opinions that are compelling without the need to resort to coercion. Children, even very young children, are not stupid or naturally irrational.

Autonomous educators, however, do think that children can become irrational, (as irrational as many adults are), when they are constantly subjected to coercion. This 'thinking' damage is hard to prove, (as hard as the converse view would be to prove), as it is not something that can be subjected to rigorous scientific investigation. But the theory that coercion causes damage to children's thinking processes is logically sustainable. A child who is constantly coerced to tidy a room is likely to build up a store of resentment about tidying in general and may always have mental blocks to the whole idea of tidying. A child who is forced to eat certain foods may grow up with irrational aversions, or even, where the coercion is more general and prolonged, develop irrational behaviours around food or eating disorders. A child who learns that doing a maths worksheet will postpone or even dispense with the requirement to wash dishes cannot think about maths in an objectively rational sense without some clouding of judgement occurring. Systematic coercion that covers all area of children's lives is even more devastating. Many children are told what they 'must' and 'must not' do. For example, not watch certain kinds of TV, not go to bed after 9 p.m., not play computer games when they 'should' be reading a book. Moreover, this detailed control and instruction is justified as being for 'their own benefit'. Any rebellion, which they feel, must therefore be an indicator of their own wrong-mindedness and self-destruction. A child who is used to a regime of coercion 'for her own good' is highly unlikely to grow up with a belief in her own capacity for rational, creative and original thinking. Rather she will mistrust her own thoughts in favour of the often irrational ideas that have been constantly forced upon her, repeating the same ideas with the same assumptions that children are in no position to argue when they become parents themselves.

Autonomous education, on the other hand, assumes that all ideas should be subject to scrutiny. An autonomously educated child told to brush her teeth every night will be able to weigh the argument on its merits rather than because it emanates from a source of authority. Autonomy respecting adults will also take care to ensure that they give information with as much honesty to which they themselves have access. Thus the parent advising teeth brushing would not mislead the child by saying that massive tooth decay will result from varying the time of brushing or from missing some brushings. They might explain that genetic factors will have a bearing on how strong the child's teeth are. Children who know that they are consistently being given a true picture so far as their admittedly fallible parents know it, will have no reason to develop irrational theories of their own.

A lifestyle choice

Those pursuing autonomy in their relationships do so based on certain theories. Coercion damages thinking and particularly robs children of their own intrinsic motivations. Lines of demarcation between what is and is not educational have to be eradicated. The result, for those who embark on this process, is that autonomous education soon becomes a total lifestyle choice. This is certainly what autonomously home educating parents have themselves noted,

"Lots of our home educating friends don't have TVs and a few don't have videos either. I have certainly had that fear that children with unlimited access to this medium will 'do nothing' else or that somehow their creativity and time will all be sapped away, but the more I have let go of my irrational fear the more I have been proved wrong.

"The things the children watch spark off stories, artwork, incredibly complicated fantasy games and some of our best and most profound discussions. Films have a way of raising issues that make the children ask questions and ignite their

curiosity. The same topics would seem cold, dry and artificial if just introduced by their father or myself without any context."

Another parent writes,

"The other positive spin-off of autonomous education has been in the tidying up department. This is an area I have difficulty dealing rationally with. Over the years I've wasted massive amounts of emotional energy and countless hours of the children's time because of my own irrational ideas about tidiness and it never achieved anything but hurt feelings and mounting levels of irrationality in everyone else. Re-ordering the spaces in our home has meant that the playroom is completely invisible to me and the children's rooms have become much more their private territory. All the hassle about tidying up has disappeared.

"This is a crucial educational step for us because we firmly believe that coercing children only damages their thinking processes and ability to remain rational and creative, so whatever coercion we can eliminate from their lives can only help them to be the wonderfully rational, creative people they really are."

Another parent puts it like this,

"It took some time for us to see that it was not a switch from one place of educational delivery (school) to another (home) but a total paradigm shift. Education has become, for us, a way of life that has nothing to do with imparting facts or covering subjects and everything to do with each family member exploring his or her own growth and development according to his or her own intrinsic values and goals, with other family members supporting the endeavour. The shift in thinking is so radical that we have found it increasingly impossible to limit the effects of unschooling to one area of life."

The flexibility that comes with autonomous education is a common thread,

"We don't have to have bedtime set so that the children can get up for school; my son can wear his favourite stripey top until it falls apart; hair can be any style, any colour; but the best part is that we are all learning, all of the time, having to

take apart fundamental assumptions and taking each others'
opinions into consideration."

Another common thread is the demise of artificial barriers between
areas of life that may once have been demarcated as educational or
not educational,

"Life and learning are inseparable. If the learning
environment is based on autonomy, it would be hypocritical to
maintain that children have the intelligence and ability to
determine what they learn, but not when to go to bed. They
will learn when it is best for themselves to go to bed, etc.
without our preconceived notions."

Or again,

"I don't see a separation between autonomy for a child in
'learning' and in other aspects of his/her life. It is a matter of
respecting children's ownership of their own life in every
aspect. The child growing up in this way, respects the
autonomy of everyone else and therefore life can be more
harmonious."

To those who have become accustomed to the impact of
autonomous education on their family life-style, it can seem
patently obvious that we cannot judge when thinking or learning is
taking place in someone else's mind, and it is therefore essential to
allow autonomy to flourish in every area of life if we truly value
education. It is also the case, however, that parents are fallible and
are likely to have their own quirks of irrational thinking from the
coercion they have previously sustained in their own lives. This
being the case it is quite common for families to embark on an
autonomous approach without having worked through the
implications for lifestyle or even to try to hold onto certain areas of
control whilst giving an increased level of academic freedom.

There is certainly no consensus on what parents 'should' retain
control of, whether they are coming from an authoritarian or liberal
position, but certain areas of autonomy recur over and over again as
common sticking points. The topics included here are not
exhaustive, but merely pointers to how irrational thinking and
unexamined assumptions can close down areas of autonomy unless
we are prepared to question everything.

Common limits on autonomy

Television is frequently sited as being addictive, passive, detrimental to creativity and likely to foster antisocial attitudes, even to the extent of extreme violence. It is, therefore, regularly something that is put beyond the bounds of children's autonomy with no television existing in the home. Alternatively, restrictions are placed on viewing, either overtly, in the form of time limitations or programme censorship or, more subtly, by communicating strong disapproval of certain programmes or genres.

Food is another area of coercion that is sometimes restricted without thought of how this restricts education in general. This is particularly the case when the food in question is high in sugar content or comes under the pejorative label of 'junk'. An example of this kind of split thinking was recently very apparent in an advert in the national *Education Otherwise* magazine when a parent advertised for like-minded people who would, "*allow their children to be self-directed*", but added that the aim was to create a "*... sugar/sweet-free environment for both us, as parents/guardians, and our children*" in which everyone could, "*...choose what we want to do and learn...*" (p.30 Issue 127).

Types of play are often at least discouraged if not altogether banned; gun play or role-play that includes any fantasy of violence often meets with cajoling to stop or distaste. Computer games are often accused of causing mood changes in children in order to justify regulation or outright censorship.

Another area that many of those who would happily call themselves 'unschoolers' often see as a sticking point or 'boundary issue' is that of safety. Even amongst many who allow for self-directed learning there is a fear that without mechanical rules children are liable to do themselves harm, even to the point of fatal injury.

Of course, these issues and others such as bedtimes or teeth brushing etcetera, are broadly parenting issues. In terms of autonomous education, however, it is crucial that they are also seen in the light of their impact on education. Both because restrictions in these areas have inevitable effects on thinking and creativity, and because limiting autonomy in these spheres also has the deleterious effect of creating a hierarchy of learning that militates against true self-direction.

One parent who had recently begun to home educate and was keen to adopt an autonomous approach wrote about her relief and pride when her daughter decided to write a story after some days spent mostly playing a computer game. Although this parent espoused self-direction and had not actually interfered with the game-playing he had certainly communicated his value system to his daughter and had thus exerted a subtle pressure on his daughter to choose certain activities in order to gain approval.

It is often over these 'lifestyle' issues that autonomous education becomes a casualty of parental irrational fears and control. Many parents would espouse a child-led education, but only whilst the content of that education remains, at least, loosely associated with the standard curriculum mentality. Thus the children remain in control whilst they are choosing reading or maths or history activities, and even whilst they are viewing specifically educational TV, using CD ROMs marketed for their educational content, or building Lego models.

Fewer parents, however, maintain the value of autonomy when the child becomes fascinated by a particular soap opera, the genre of action movies or CD ROMs full of strategy and fantasy violence. It is much more common to assume that such material is not only not educational, but actively damaging of creativity and even of morality. This is the very antithesis of the theory I proposed above, that any interference with autonomy undermines the thinking processes and sabotages just that intrinsic motivation which is crucial to real education.

The question arises, therefore, can a child be autonomously educated and have restrictions placed on their TV viewing and computer game-playing? The answer must be 'no'. It cannot be pretended that the child has autonomy if these kinds of limits are place on it. Yet many parents still continue to ask whether such limits on autonomy are none-the-less justifiable and reasonable. Are they a necessary and even helpful boundary on an otherwise child led pattern of learning? Is the trade off between a slight lack of autonomy and increased protection a good one?

There are certainly parents who would describe themselves as autonomous home educators who would never-the-less prevent, or at least discourage, certain levels or types of TV watching and computer games. There are also autonomously home educating parents who share strong theories with their children in the belief that TV is addictive, destroys creativity, creates lethargy or increases aggression, (or even, despite the contradiction, does both of the latter).

Switching on the television and computer

Parents who continue to suspect that television viewing and playing computer games are 'bad' activities have plenty of company as a recent article in the New York Times demonstrated.   Denise Caruso, in an article entitled, *Linking Entertainment to Violence* referred to a growing body of evidence of the effects of violent TV on children,

> *"Hundreds of studies in recent decades have revealed a direct correlation between exposure to media violence - now including video games - and increased aggression."*

Caruso goes on to link TV and games with, 'psychological techniques of desensitization, conditioning and vicarious learning'. She sites 'evidence' that recent young killers such as Michael Carneal, the 14-year-old boy who opened fire on a prayer group in a school foyer in 1997, and the boys who conducted the massacre at Littleton Colorado, were accomplished games players.   She fails, however, to set out any logical process of cause and effect.   Caruso sites Joel Federman, co-director of the Centre for Communication and Social Policy at the University of California at Santa Barbara, as her expert witness.   Federman published an annotated bibliography called *The Social Effects of Interactive Electronic Games*.   Yet even Federman has to acknowledge that studies have been limited and do not all agree.   The majority of these very few studies do, predictably, argue for a correlation between aggressive games and an increased likelihood of actual aggression.   But Federman jumps unjustifiably from correlation to cause, going on to likening producers of violent media to the tobacco industry in its denial of causality.   Federman concludes,

> *" ... since not every kid experiences the extreme effects, people can continue to deny them."* (Copyright 1999, *The New York Times Company)*

Yet this is precisely the point of the counter argument.   We have some correlation, perhaps, but that does not add up to cause.   What is it in the life of the children who go on to offend, or even kill, that is the common causative thread?   Those who favour an autonomous approach to education would argue that the common thread is not TV or computer games, but coercion.   It is the systematic destruction of a child's ability to think rationally and control his or her life and learning that leads to antisocial and violent behaviours. These children are alienated from themselves, their peers and their communities not because of a violent strategy game or an action movie, no matter how intense the exposure, but because they have come from situations of coercion. It might be coercion by neglect, having endured years of lack of parental engagement, or they may have been subject to systematic extrinsic control of some or all areas of their lives. The fact that not all children experience the 'same extreme effects' is because aggression is not an effect of TV watching and game playing, rather the TV watching and game playing in a particularly isolated manner were themselves just other symptoms of the 'extreme' coercion.

I recently engaged in a discussion about TV viewing with a mother who claimed that she had been made 'lazy' by being brought up in home where the TV was permanently on and where TV was her parents' main priority. This mother's contention was that TV would therefore damage her children's ability to think and be motivated unless she restricted their viewing. It was interesting that this mother firmly blamed television when in fact the blame lay with her parents. I pointed out that I grew up in a similar home and rather than becoming lazy had reacted by become academically industrious and as different as possible from my parents. In neither case was the television the cause of laziness or academic industry. In both cases, parental neglect, a form of coercion, had had effects on our thinking.

Television is an object. It is a source of learning in so many areas of thinking. It delivers information quickly and in a form that is eminently   digestible.   Video   games   provide   stimulating entertainment and build up a vast store of knowledge about problem solving. Yet, parents are suspicious. Why? In an interview between Sarah Lawrence and David Deutsch, Deutsch asked,

> *"Why do so many adults hate them?   What **evidence** is there that there is anything bad about them?*
>
> *"If you look at it closely, the evidence boils down to no more than the fact that children **like** video games.   There seems to be a very common tendency among parents to regard children **liking** something as **prima facie** evidence that it is bad for them. If they are spending a lot of time doing something, parents wonder what harm it must be doing them. I think this is fundamentally the wrong attitude.*

*"The right attitude is: if children are spending a lot of time doing something, let's try to find ways of letting them do **even more** of it. **Prima facie**, the fact that they like doing it is an indication that it is good for them.*

"I think that overwhelmingly the thing which draws people's attention to video games is the fact that children like them. People jump from that solitary piece of evidence to the conclusion that there must be something wrong with video games!"

Deutsch goes on to defend video games,

"They provide a unique learning environment. They provide something which for most of human history was not available, namely, an interactive complex entity that is accessible at low cost and zero risk.

*"Let's compare video games with other great educational things in the world. Books and television have great complexity and diversity - they give you access to almost every aspect of human culture and knowledge - but they are not interactive. On the other hand, something like playing the piano is also complex, and interactive, but it requires an enormous initial investment (months or years of practice or training) with the associated huge risk of misplacing that investment. One cannot make many such investments in one's life. I should say, of course, that **the** most educational thing in the world is conversation. That does have the property that it is complex, interactive, and ought to have a low cost, although often between children and adults it has a high cost and high risk for the children, but it should not and need not.*

Apart from conversation, all the complex interactive things require a huge initial investment, except video games, and I think video games are a breakthrough in human culture for that reason. They are not some transient, fringe aspect of culture; they are destined to be an important means of human learning for the rest of history, because of this interactive element. Why is being interactive so important? Because interacting with a complex entity is what life and thinking and creativity and art and science are all about."

In answer to Lawrence's query about the amount of time a child might spend on video games Deutsch says,

"First, how do you know what the appropriate number of hours is? Nobody can know that. If your children were playing chess for several hours a day, you would boast about what geniuses they are. There is no intrinsic difference between chess and a video game, or indeed, even between things like playing the piano and playing video games, except that playing the piano has this enormous initial cost.

"They are similar kinds of activity. One of them is culturally sanctioned and the other is still culturally stigmatised, but for no good reason. I spent a lot of time playing with Lego when I was a child. For some reason, it never occurred to my parents that because I spent hours and hours with Lego, this was bad for me. If it had occurred to them, they could have done a lot of harm. I know now, for myself, that the thing which makes me play video games today is identical to the thing which made me play with Lego then - which is, by the way, the very same thing that makes me do science - that is, the impulse to understand things."

Deutsch recognises that for a child who is generally unhappy computer games could become an escape route, but this does not make the games bad in themselves. It is better, of course, if the child is helped to find multiple outlets for his creativity which he genuinely prefers, but taking away the child's *"last remaining source of joy and learning"* is not a solution and Deutsch goes on,

"On the whole, if we are talking about how the overwhelming majority of children interact with video games, the reason they sit in front of them for hours is that they are very valuable things to sit in front of. The skills they are learning are needed in every creative aspect of life, and children will always be short of opportunities to learn them. The natural and healthy state of human beings is that we are constantly looking for opportunities to improve our thinking skills, to improve the complexity and the subtlety of the mental apparatus which we apply to the world. Traditionally, this has been expensive, but people still did it. Even learning to play chess is expensive, compared with learning to play a video game. The expense does not make it any more moral. It is a disadvantage of chess or playing the piano that they have this initial cost.

*"... The benefit of a video game is not that you learn the video game; it is that you learn the mental skills **with which** you are learning the video game, and **those** skills are good for learning **anything**."*

In terms of the violence Deutsch points out that there is a lot more to modern computer games than mere shooting,

"The most popular types of games nowadays are platform games, whose basic themes are exploring, jumping around, finding and collecting things (though admittedly one usually has to fight the occasional monster on the way), and completely abstract games such as Tetris."

More pertinently, he adds,

"Violence is where you hurt people. Games just appear on a screen; they don't actually hurt anybody. The only actual hurting that goes on is by parents when they prevent or discourage children from playing.

*"All games need an object and, if there are people in the game, it is natural to have drama, which means there will be goodies and baddies. The same is true in all drama, in all novels, plays, films, or whatever. If King Lear were the first play a person had seen, he might come out severely shocked. But once you know what a play is, have seen a bit of Shakespeare and know what it is about, you know that King Lear is not actually dangerous, that people don't go around after seeing King Lear, plucking people's eyes out. People are not harmed by seeing King Lear if they have reached the stage of wanting to see it gradually, at their own pace, for their own reasons, under their own control. Video games are **par excellence** a learning environment that is under one's own control, and that prevents them from being harmful."*

(Extracts from TCS web-site copyright TCS, *Video Games: Harmfully Addictive or a Unique Educational Environment?* The web-site article is a slightly modified version of a 1992 article from *Taking Children Seriously* issue 4, 'An interview with David Deutsch', by Sarah Lawrence.)

Many of the arguments about video games also apply to TV watching. Television does not have the same interactive component as do video games, but it does have the advantage of being an incredibly diverse source of easily accessed information.

Moreover, it is a deeply effective medium for communicating culture and a fascinating source of information on how the world and people operate. Fears about a child watching 'inappropriate material', (usually anything which is deemed to have a sexual or violent content), are simply based on asking the wrong question. How can we get from assuming that children are born innately rational, trustworthy and good to believing that if given a TV they will instantly become irrational, self-destructive and bad? Children in non-coercive homes will choose to watch the things which further the learning that only they can know is going on in their own minds. They will choose content which has meaning to them, which helps them explore the questions they are ready to explore, which can be safely and fruitfully followed up in conversations with parents and other trusted adults. 'Appropriate' viewing is whatever fits into this category.

Similarly, fears about a child 'copying' bad behaviour from television programmes is an area which is as subjective as it is emotive. As a parent of three young children I was totally convinced that television watching was not only addictive, a waste of time and, for the most part, not educational. Furthermore, I was quite sure that I could observe adverse results from television watching; everything from a state of 'zombification' to excessive aggressive energy.

Interestingly, I made these observations at a time when my children's viewing was tightly restricted and there was overt disapproval of anything with the merest hint of violence. I could not be argued with. What I saw was what I saw. Some years on, as a parent of four children, I live in a home with four televisions and three video players. There are no limits on the time that can be spent watching television and there is no censorship of genre, either overt or subtle. I observe people of all ages having times when they watch a lot of television and times when they do not. I observe an enormous rise in conversational flow and breadth. I observe no addiction or 'zombification'. I observe no aggression arising from viewing levels or type of material. What has changed? Coercion.

Television does not exert negative influences, it is a neutral object, but imposing coercive restrictions around its use causes irrationality. Denying someone access to the information, ideas and entertainment that television provides cuts off a whole arena of intrinsically motivated learning. It can never be for the child's own good. For a parent to take away a child's autonomy and behave as though the child is too irrational or stupid or bad to make her own decisions, based on hearing all the theories, can only interfere with the child's growth of knowledge.

Playing their own games

When I first became a parent, and probably even before then, I knew that I would not have children who engaged in certain kinds of play, especially gun play. Thirteen years later not only have I been proved wrong, but I am happy to have been so. Gun play, war play, interest in castles or armour or military technology is not about glorifying violence or not caring about real hurt. It is a way of acting outing fantasies of good and bad, sorting out questions of how people relate or how things work. It is entertainment and information, not an early sign of psychopathic leanings and children are eminently aware that it is play, not reality.

It is not uncommon for parents to view children playing at war or showing signs of passionate interest in military paraphernalia as being in the grip of some kind of obsessive spell. The use of the word 'obsessive' is as a pejorative. I would guess that a parent with a child who spent ten hours a day or more practising a musical instrument or solving maths problems would not think of it as an obsession. It would more likely be called a consuming passion or primary interest.

Banning weapon-based toys from the house is another common practice. Children may be told that there is nothing wrong with them for being interested in them, but none-the-less denied access to such play. An area of passionate interest that cannot be satisfied must be extraordinarily frustrating and likely to lead to the desire increasing along with a host of resentments. Children are not stupid. If their parents ban certain toys they will be well aware that their parents do think there is something deeply wrong with them for having this interest. Telling them otherwise cannot compensate for behaviour to the contrary. Parents need to ask themselves what is it that they fear, either now or in the future, from a plastic gun or a plastic sword.

Ultimately, we cannot ban thoughts. Little John will go on thinking about his interest, perhaps in much less healthy ways, if he constantly has to fantasise about what it might be like to play with guns and swords, video war strategy games and fantasy figures and all the other things he could be learning from. Allowing for other outlets for aggression is no compensation. We cannot know what learning is taking place in another's mind from a given activity and a child who wants to pursue his learning through gun play might very well be gaining knowledge which has absolutely nothing to do with aggression.   On the other hand, a child whose play and learning is thwarted will be learning a lot about aggression and self-doubt. I have no personal taste for weaponry, but I could never be sure that another's passion for these toys could lead only in evil or tragic directions. On the contrary, what might a child's passion lead him to invent? What incredible empathy might be being developed?

What we have to decide is whether we believe children to be basically good, rational and trustworthy. If we do then we should not be in the business of compromising their autonomy. Their play is a powerful engine of learning.

Junk, mess and manners

What have eating so-called junk foods, (burgers, sweets and cola seem to be the leading bogeys), not wanting to live in a pristine bedroom, mechanically saying 'please' and 'thank you' or brushing teeth religiously, got to do with education? When we are talking about autonomous education, the answer is everything, so long as they remain issues of coercion which sabotage the basic engine of intrinsic motivation.

This is not, primarily, a parenting book, but the arguments which apply to video games, television and play, beyond that which would normally be deemed as 'educational' apply equally in these spheres. A coerced mind is not one that is learning optimally. I am not suggesting lives of endless self-sacrifice for parents, but I am suggesting that the solutions which are reached in any given family must be mutually preferred by all parties. Neither am I suggesting a situation of neglectful license. This will often involve participants in changing their theories in order to adopt new and better ones.

Surprisingly, it is often theories like, 'there are good foods and bad foods', 'untidiness is a sign of moral laxity' and 'all teeth need two doses of fluoride a day' that begin to be questioned. Parents embarking on non-coercive education learn to question everything and to realise that mechanical rules are inimical to a family where creativity and true learning are highly prized. (To explore the relationship between these issues further you can find more information on the *Taking Children Seriously* web-site at www.tcs.ac)

Education, education and education

The government claims to have 'Education, Education and Education' as a top priority. Autonomous educators claim that this is impossible within the confines of an extrinsically motivated system populated, by and large, by coerced children who do not want to be there. In contrast they present the possibility of flexible family lifestyles in which every aspect of personal autonomy is respected, nurtured and facilitated in order to enable the most unhindered growth of knowledge possible.

Chapter seven

Evidence without evaluation

Escaping curricula thinking

The schooling world, and those parts of the home educating world which are a pale reflection of it, are obsessed with evaluating and monitoring children's progress. The pressure on home educating families to conform to such monitoring is enormous and can be made to seem innocuous when in fact it is intrusive and destructive of the learning process. Autonomously educating parents are often caught in a seemingly impossible situation. They are required by law to educate their children and there may be times when they are called on to give evidence that education is taking place. Sadly, this is too often taken to mean that evidence is synonymous with producing children's work for scrutiny, supplying timetables, plans and diaries of completed work or even subjecting children to unwanted testing and questioning.

Evidence is not synonymous with any of these things, but only has to be some supporting information that on the balance of probabilities would lead a reasonable person to agree that an education is taking place, (see Appendix 1 for the legal details). The lure to go further than that is highly detrimental to autonomous learning. But it often comes with enormous pressure, whether from authorities or from friends and neighbours who believe that evaluation beyond what is legally required is for the children's ubiquitous and iniquitous 'own good'.

The need to satisfy an LEA officer with 'evidence' can sometimes be the trigger for panic measures which interfere with and damage the autonomous process of education. It can be at such moments that we allow ourselves to go 'curriculum browsing', causing our children's education to become an object under scrutiny, fragmented from the integrity of every day living with all the resultant effects on the children's thinking. It is under the pressure to produce evidence, (often in forms which we are not reasonably or legally obliged to give), that we can shift our focus from an individual, unique child to a system which is, at best, woefully poor and, at worst, actively destructive. It is then that we can become caught up with external motivation and performance.

Why would autonomous educators fall into this trap? Because the ideology of the curriculum as **the** yardstick of how we value and interact with our children is pervasive. Almost every time the new school term starts I am inundated with questions about whether our children are 'back to lessons' yet; even by other home educators who know that we do not hold with transmissive notions of education. More worryingly, I recently heard one teacher espousing the view that any reasonable LEA officer can judge whether a child is being legally educated only by comparing his or her 'progress' with peers being taught the National Curriculum. Sadly the many horror stories concerning the behaviour of some LEA officers prove that this teacher is far from alone in his thinking that proof of education means proof of school-defined agendas being force-fed to all children, whether in or out of school.

Authorities, friends, relatives, other home educators who are more formal in their approach, and a media which constantly talks about children in terms of standards and value added, as though they were just another consumable product, all press upon us. We are, therefore, unlikely to be able to so far remove ourselves from the world that the whispers will not ever creep in and disturb us. In the face of all this we are going to survive only if we are well stocked with tactics which support what for most people is a crazy and extremist view of education and pedagogy.

We first need to be clear in our own thinking. What purpose does a curriculum serve? The whole process of defining, implementing and managing a curriculum is related to standardisation and control. It is not so much a tool of education as a tool for the management of large, artificially created groups. Our society is not one that likes or respects children. Children are seen as a problem to be solved, and schools and the curricula that fill the school days are part of the management solution. Schools, no matter how small, are centred on groups and systems, not individuals. A curriculum is so designed not because it presents the right things at the right time. It is preposterous to imagine that it must be the right time for all children in a class aged from six to seven years to learn to tell the time on a particular Friday in October. A curriculum so designed is to do the best it can to manage the diverse needs of a huge range of children who are artificially brought together on the basis of one arbitrary factor - their age by any given September.

So why should we ever need to consult such curricula even for ideas of what might interest our children? We do not need to. The world is full to bursting with all sorts of sources of information and learning in so many media. With access to all of this, we need only to consult our children and go where they lead. The key is to notice our children's clues as to what direction they want to take, and give them all the help they want in taking it. Curricula are for institutions, not for creative people. We need to get that message ingrained in our own psyches so that we can resist all the atrocious but pervasive theories about how much our children are missing out on by not studying for level 2 SATs tests!

We also need to be clear about why commonly accepted notions of monitoring and progress are so damaging and futile. The notion of 'progress' is such a tempting one. It can so readily be 'shown' that children, (that is children who are being coercively school children), do gain satisfaction in this way. This is only, however, because they have learnt from the painful experience of having their work judged as good or bad, as progressing or failing, that the only way to get the attention and approval that all children should have by right is to play the progress game. The satisfaction is a vicarious one and not a joy in the learning itself. Learning is not a self-fulfilling pleasure, but an object with which to court affection and notice. Autonomous creative children do not need any artificial means of knowing that they are constantly developing and learning. We do not commonly tape-record baby noises so that our ten-year-olds can compare how far their speech has come and be congratulated for it. We trust that our babies will talk, that our children will learn an amazing range of skills and knowledge and that they do not need to be patronised by having their so-called 'progress' pointed out to them.

The related notion of monitoring is similarly based on inadequate theories. We know from general experience that the process of discovery always affects what is being discovered. There is no such thing as neutral observation. If we think that we can keep a secret diary or portfolio, we are fooling ourselves. Aside from the implications this has for the respect between parents and children, it would be virtually impossible not to allow the monitoring to have some coercive and/or objectifying effect on the process of autonomous learning.

Our first tactic then is to know our arguments. It is so commonly assumed that curriculum, progress and monitoring are beneficial that we can easily be sucked into the pervasive and oppressive mentality unless we are standing on firm theoretical ground. These things are not good for children; they are attempts to control how, what and when children should learn and they are to be resisted.

We gave up record-keeping a long time ago, having come to feel that it was not simply an innocuous safety net of evidence, but rather an intrusive mechanism that changed process into product (artificially) and made negative and (to us) wrong distinctions about what counted as education. For example, we might record a painting or a book being read, but not bath-time or lying on the sofa gazing at the ceiling for an hour. Yet, in fact we could not know which of those experiences was actually educational in the sense of being inside someone else's head where the learning was taking place. Much of learning does not lend itself directly to evidence except in indirect asides and, even then, often much later and in other contexts. (The above argument is adapted from an article I wrote for *TCS*, issue 24, 'Tactics for non-coercive education'.)

Children are not products

True education is not an issue of performance. Measurements of progress are merely coercive bribes, which artificially freeze our images of who our children are on one particular snapshot of time. We would do better to cease from thinking of our children as products. On the *TCS* mailing list a succession of writers have developed the very useful image of the iceberg, an enormous entity which is constantly evolving and largely hidden from view.

> *"So I think of people as huge icebergs. When I look at my child and focus in on one aspect of him, I recognize that what I am seeing is not the 'whole' person by any stretch of the imagination. It is only the part of the iceberg that happens to be above water and visible right now, or that I happen to be focusing upon. I am then better able to be aware that my perception is far from accurate or the 'whole picture', it is only my interpretation of a small aspect of the person based on very very limited information - how can it be anything else when the bulk of that person is totally invisible to me?"*

The image of the iceberg is an enormously helpful one in ridding ourselves of the tendency to label our children as successes or failures or to see them in any way as products of our parenting or education. It frees us from the need to construct our child as a perfect product and, instead, allows us to realise that what we see of another person is simply what is visible at that time. All we ever have is our own limited perception of a constant and dynamic process.

If our children are not products, then what does it matter that at any one moment a child is consumed with a particular subject to the exclusion of all else; that the child has not 'done' any maths this week or is allegedly exceeding so called peer levels in geography? In a school environment these things matter because of the operation of an artificial environment with a determination to inflict homogeneity of learning and behaviour. This environment can be totally dispensed with in a home education setting where only the child's intrinsic motivation and autonomy govern what is learned. In autonomous home education, the need to keep taking learning's temperature is superfluous. The need to define and objectify the child is meaningless. One *TCS* poster adds,

> *"Of course the knowledge that 'whatever is visible of the iceberg' is very much simply a matter of what I choose to see and how I choose to see it - that even looking at just what is above the surface is very 'non-definite' - it is just my interpretation and is very subjective - is important too."*

In a lifetime, we are lucky if we come to understand ourselves well. Even if we do achieve this, we never really know the whole. It is presumptuous and demeaning to think that we can know another. We make observations, always partial, even if sometimes helpful, but it is not reasonable, helpful or necessary to coerce a child by constantly barraging him with evaluation. The only question that remains is, 'how can I as a parent help my child to do the things he wants with his life in ways that will not impose anyone's agenda but his own, in ways that will not seek to define or control or modify my child against his will?'

Presenting evidence

So where does this leave the business of evidence? This should not need intrusive visits, requests for pieces of work or diaries, which make artificial distinctions between subjects or what does and does not have educational content. What is relevant is the parents' commitment to ensuring that children have every opportunity to pursue whatever it is they want to pursue for as long as it is relevant to the child.

Autonomously educating parents are serious about the education of their children and, as such, have nothing to fear from the demands of providing a legal education. The burden of any evidence which they submit to local education authorities is likely to rest in a full statement of their educational philosophy. This sets out their serious intent to follow section 7 of the 1996 Education Act, that parents should ensure that their children receive efficient full-time education suitable to their age, ability, and aptitude, and to any special educational needs they may have. Such a report can fully demonstrate that since life and learning are inherently of a piece in autonomous education then all of waking time (and perhaps even sleeping time) is spent on education. Such a report would be in keeping with educational law in having no concept of attempting to cause a child to know any particular essentials, but rather of ensuring that education is 'efficient'.

A child learning something to suit his or her own intrinsic and individual purposes is surely the most efficient form of education possible, given that 'efficient' has been defined as achieving 'that which it sets out to achieve'. As long as children remain the prime movers in their own learning then it is more than possible to assert that efficient education is taking place. The requirements of age, ability and aptitude, (which would also pertain to any special needs), have been dealt with in chapter four above and any report written to satisfy LEAs will need to take these factors into account as they relate to their autonomous education.

A well written report detailing educational philosophy and provision, without recourse to compromising children's privacy or turning their education into an objectified product, should be sufficient to satisfy any reasonable person that on the balance of probabilities a serious education is being embarked on in the homes of autonomously educating parents. Sadly this is too often not the case. Writing on an internet mailing list for home educators a representative of the leading national home educators support organisation, *Education Otherwise*, wrote,

> *"Several members of the EO council will be meeting soon with a DfEE representative to discuss a number of issues.*

> *"One of the things which we are planning to discuss is the misleading and/or inaccurate statements which have appeared in some leaflets issued by the DfEE.. I know that a number of these have been mentioned on this list, and it would be very helpful to have details of any that any of you know about.*

"We are also hoping to discuss how home educators perceive their relationships with LEAs, and it would be great to have details of good practice to show the DfEE representative. We already have details enough of bad practice to fill several shopping trolleys! If you feel that you have a good, supportive LEA, we would be very interested to know who they are and what makes them good. It would be particularly helpful if you have any written material from them which we could have/borrow like information leaflets or forms."

There was only one response and that was not glowing. In contrast, the list regularly features horror stories of LEAs who bluntly refuse to accept evidence in anything other than their favoured form of home visits with interviews of the children. Home visits are not compulsory and the choice not to have them is not prima facie evidence of inadequate educational provision. Good legal advice can be a supportive starting point where more is being required than is legally necessary and the home educators' co-operative, *Choice in Education*, now has an excellent expert legal team.   When parents decide that it is in their best interests to submit additional evidence, (and this must be a carefully weighed decision if it is not to be the start of merely paying Danegeld!), a number of avenues remain open. Meetings can be on neutral territory and a friend and a tape recorder are often helpful elements in a meeting. If an LEA officer is invited into a private home it can be made clear that the meeting is for a particular time and should stay within legal guidelines. Children do not have to be present at any such meetings and, if they decide they would prefer to be present, should not be interrogated or tested. If the family feel that presenting examples of 'work' is likely to lead to detrimental objectification of the educational process, they might prefer to ask other friends, particularly those with some educational status in the eyes of the local education authority. They should write supporting reports on their own reflections of the educational provision. These can even be made as legal affidavits where the need for such is felt to be pressing.

Not following the dominant system of education does not mean that evidence is lacking. It may mean that those with a particular mentality find it harder to conceive of this. It may require extra commitment to guarding the autonomy that is so highly prized. It may sometimes involve long negotiations or seeking outside advice, but ultimately, autonomous educators can be confident that they are fulfilling the law and have nothing to fear from it because they take education very seriously indeed.

Chapter eight

Autonomy as a life-long process

Moving into the world

Autonomous education is always part of a process within the wider community. It is a process that happens over a whole lifetime. Just as autonomous educators do not make artificial distinctions between what counts as education and what does not, neither do they see education as something that is about a particular period of childhood. Just as there are unwarranted fears over the social skills of autonomously educated children, so there are corresponding but equally unwarranted fears about how they will fit into the world, coming, as they do, from such different educational and experiential backgrounds.

Those who choose their own education and are serious in their pursuit of independent, self-directed learning are highly likely to be just the sort of creative, flexible, resourceful young people that a post-modernist society should and will welcome. This has certainly been the finding of Julie Webb in her recent publication, *Those Unschooled Minds: home-educated children grow up*, (Educational Heretics Press, 1999). Webb notes that children's ability to organise their own education brings with it a flexibility that is often critical in later career developments. Take, for example, the case of Laurence, who went on to study at Cambridge before launching his own web-site design business (p.18). Webb also notes that there tends to be a strong emphasis on creativity, which again has bearings on later paths. She cites the case of Harriet who began working as a puppeteer at the age of twelve and Grace who developed a career in music, including a PhD (p.22).

Webb remarks that all those in her study retained an emphasis on lifelong learning, (p.24), and did not have set ideas about ages at which things could be learned. Two participants, for example, took up language learning as young adults and another began to play the cello in her mid-teens before going to study it at Oxford, (pp.26-27). Webb also emphasises that those who took part in her research exhibited the kind of range of social activity and lifestyle as adults as would be observed in any random group of people in their twenties and thirties, (p.54). Two major aspects of their lives, which she noted, were a tendency for a high degree of input into the community and continuing good relationships with parents as adults, (p.57).

In terms of the world of work, Webb found that home-educated young people commonly began experiences of work before the age of 16 and were open to trying out many options, (p.60). Very few of her participants settled into one job at an early age, but exhibited a breadth of flexibility and creativity, (p.63). Many used voluntary work as a base for experience, (p.65). Those who had been home-educated were very adaptable and able to switch paths easily if one avenue did not work out, (p.67). As Webb summed up, the group being studied,

> "... embrace modern uncertainty and all its possibilities with enthusiasm, feeling themselves well equipped to take advantage of whatever changing opportunities ... might come their way." (p.71)

Webb's study did not look exclusively at autonomously home-educated young people. She did identify, however, certain factors as being of significance in the group's understanding of lifelong learning and their own abilities to manage complex life choices. Learners having control over the educational content and timing of their learning; the stress on flexibility, adaptability and creativity and an openness to acquire learning in many different environments within the community were all key factors which are particularly to be found in autonomous education. Far from finding it more difficult to fit into the world, whether in the spheres of higher education or work of all types, it should be the case that a childhood in which autonomy has always been the key, is most suited to an adult life lived with maximum creativity and flexibility. Non-coercive education lays a constant stress on problem solving and on the continual possibility of conjecture and refutation leading to new and better theories and practice. It is, therefore, in an eminent position to foster adults who continue to believe positively that solutions exist and that choices remain open.

In a world where there are fewer and fewer jobs for life and where change is likely to be rapid, being accustomed to thinking independently and engaging continually in problem solving are likely to lead to young adults who have many fewer problems than their schooled counterparts in managing their own futures.

In conclusion

Autonomous education is a valid system of education, which allows children and young people to develop the lifelong habit of being self-directed and intrinsically motivated learners. It is a process that looks remarkably unlike what we expect to see of education, but none-the-less withstands the criticisms of its practice and holds up well as educational theory.

Autonomous education, like the epistemology of Karl Popper, takes as its premise the idea of instruction from within. It is a system of education that can find support in the fields of education, philosophy and psychology. It is coherent, defensible and gaining ground, with an increasing number of advocates and practitioners.

Autonomous education takes as its moral and philosophical premise the right of self-government and free will. Education is the process by which we develop intellectually as our knowledge grows and it relies on the rational development of conjecture and refutation. Autonomous education is simply that process by which knowledge grows because of the intrinsic motivation of the individual. In fact, the core to understanding autonomous education is the primacy of intrinsic motivation. Whilst various learning methods might be employed, with the constructivist model being the most likely contender in many situations, it is always and only intrinsic motivation which is fundamental.

Autonomous education, in addition to being centred in the child's intrinsic motivation, demands a broad definition of education. There should be a step back from the products and outcomes thinking of conventional education, a positive view of children as creative and rational and an ability to conceive of problems as having solutions. Many who follow an autonomous path may begin with ideas of following what is natural and even of imparting some untainted natural or mystical nature to children. Others come from an unschooling position that focuses on autonomy within areas defined as 'educational'. The requirement, however, to aver from coercion or any extrinsic motivation, (no matter how good it seems in itself), pushes the truly autonomous educator beyond the frameworks of romanticised thinking or even of much unschooling thinking into the radical paradigm of **taking children seriously**.

Autonomous education does not have a list of essentials, but considers that children will learn whatever they need to live the lives they choose and they will do so at ages that suit their own particular and individual processes. The question of balance and the possibility of children doing nothing are simply meaningless.

For children growing up autonomously, socialisation is not about functionality or compliance, but within a framework of developing a strong sense of self-socialisation, is varied and positive.

Education is not something which can be demarcated from the bulk of life, but rather involves the whole of life, in both breadth and duration.   Autonomous education is a total lifestyle choice involving an adherence to the principle of eradicating coercion from family relationships.

Autonomous education is not only theoretically supportable, but also a consistent legal way for parents to discharge their duties to educate their children under section 7 of the 1996 Education Act. It is quite possible to give evidence of such education without compromising children's privacy or falling into the curriculum and product mentalities.

In short, this is a form of education that is becoming increasingly popular as more people realise that children are not containers to be filled or automatons to be switched on.   But, that they are full human beings with full moral and rational capacities deserving the kind of self determination that is due to us all. Autonomous education begins before and extends well beyond the years of government-defined 'compulsory' education, but during those years it is the optimal approach for ensuring that a process of flexible, creative, lifelong learning is set in motion.

Mark Twain once said,

> *"Soap and education are not as sudden as a massacre, but they are more deadly in the long run."*

We do not have to hand our children over to such a slow and hideous death, particularly when the alternative is so life-enhancing.

Appendix 1

Elective Home Education: Legal Guidelines
(Act numbers refer to The Education Act 1996 unless otherwise stated.)

Education is compulsory - school attendance is not
The freedom to educate children at home forms an intrinsic and essential element of educational provision in our society, a right which has been protected by a succession of Education Acts. **The law is clear that while education is compulsory, school attendance is not.**

Education law
The fundamental piece of legislation regarding education in England and Wales is the **Education Act 1996,** (a consolidating act which incorporates the 1944 Education Act and later legislation). The **only** relevant sections *(with emphasis added)* are:

Parental duties:
Section 7
> *"The parent of every child of compulsory school age shall cause him to receive efficient full-time education suitable;*
> *a) to his age, ability, and aptitude, and*
> *b) to any special educational needs he may have, either by regular attendance at school **or otherwise.**"*

LEA duties:
The LEA's duties and powers in relation to home-educated children are contained in the Education Acts, 1944 to 1996. These are fully set out in sections 437 to 443 of the 1996 Act and, (except in relation to special educational needs), are limited to the provisions of those sections.

> *"437. (1) **If it appears** to a local education authority that a child of compulsory school age in their area is not receiving suitable education, either by regular attendance at school or otherwise, they shall serve a notice in writing on the parent requiring him to satisfy them within the period specified in the notice that the child is receiving such education."*

Parental responsibilities
Under section 576 of the Education Act 1996, a parent is defined in relation to a child or young person as also including any individual:

(a) who is not a parent of his but who has parental responsibility for him, or

(b) who has care of him.

As parents are responsible for ensuring that their children are properly educated, **it is their decision** whether to use schools or provide education at home.

It is important to note that the duty to secure education is stated entirely in section 7 and nowhere else.

Provided the child is not a registered pupil at a school, the parent is bound by no other constraints. In particular, **there is no obligation**

- **to seek permission to educate 'otherwise';**
- **to take the initiative in informing the LEA;**
- **to have regular contact with the LEA;**
- **to have premises equipped to any particular standard;**
- **to have any specific qualifications;**
- **to cover the same syllabus as any school;**
- **to adopt the National Curriculum;**
- **to make detailed plans in advance;**
- **to observe school hours, days or terms;**
- **to have a fixed timetable;**
- **to give formal lessons;**
- **to reproduce school type peer group socialisation;**
- **to match school, age-specific standards.**

De-registration

The grounds on which a pupil's name must be deleted from the admission register are listed in Education (Pupil Registration) Regulations 9, 1995 [SI 1995/2089]. Under regulation 9(1)(c), a 'school-age' pupil's name is to be deleted from the admission register if:

> *"he has ceased to attend the school and the proprietor has received written notification from the parent that the pupil is receiving education otherwise than at school."*

If the parent writes to the proprietor explaining that the child is being educated at home, the school is obliged to take the child's name off the register, and the duty to secure regular attendance thus comes to an end. Since 1995 this has been an absolute legal requirement: no discretion is involved. (Under regulation 13(3), the proprietor of any state-funded school must also report the deletion of the pupil's name from the admission register to the LEA 'within ten school days'.) In this way, the legal position of a parent embarking on home-based education is the same regardless of whether or not the child has been withdrawn from a school for this purpose; i.e., the LEA is entitled to make informal enquiries of the parent(s).

The only circumstances under which **parents** are under an obligation to inform the LEA of the intention to home educate a child, concern pupils registered at a special school where parents must seek the consent of the LEA (Regulation 9(2) Education (Pupil Registration) Regulations, 1995 [SI 1995/2089]). This extra requirement is intended to allow LEAs to ensure that a child's special educational needs will continue to be provided for when the child is withdrawn from school, and not to discriminate against the choice to home educate a child with SEN. Parents should be given reasonable opportunity to show that a 'suitable' education, taking account of the child's special educational needs, can be provided at home, and should be given sufficient time and information to rectify any perceived shortcomings in their provision. If an LEA refuses its consent, a parent may appeal to the Secretary of State.

LEA duties
The wording of the Education Act 1996 requires the LEA to act **only** if something comes to its attention which gives it reason to suppose a breach of a parent's section 7 duty. It does not need to investigate any instances of home education which come to its attention unaccompanied by any grounds for suspicion that an adequate education is not taking place.

Case law, (Phillips v Brown, Divisional Court [20 June 1980, unreported] Judicial review by Lord Justice Donaldson, as he then was), has established, however, that an LEA may make **informal** enquiries of parents. Lord Donaldson said:

> "Of course such a request is not the same as a notice under s 37 (1) of the Education Act 1944 (now s 437 (1) of the 1996 Education Act) and the parents will be under no duty to comply. However it would be sensible for them to do so. If parents give no information or adopt the course ... of merely stating that they are discharging their duty without giving any details of how they are doing so, the LEA will have to consider and decide whether it 'appears' to it that the parents are in breach of s 36 (now s7 of the 1996 Education Act.)."

Determining 'suitable education'.

LEAs should bear in mind when considering the replies to such informal enquiries, (and other more formal ones, should the matter go that far), that parents taken to court for failing to comply with a School Attendance Order only have to show the court that they are providing a suitable education on **a balance of probabilities.** That is the test that LEAs must also apply. Also a court will receive any. evidence a parent produces; it will not have to be in any specified form and it will be sufficient so long as it shows that a suitable education is being given. Similarly an LEA has no power to require that information be given to it in a specified form or way.

The DfEE acknowledges this in their information leaflet entitled, *ENGLAND AND WALES EDUCATING CHILDREN AT HOME:*
"3. LEAs, however, have no automatic right of access to the parent's home. Parents may refuse a meeting in the home, if they can offer an alternative way of demonstrating that they are providing a suitable education, for example, through showing examples of work and agreeing to a meeting at another venue."

Another 'example' might be information provided in written form, sufficiently comprehensive to establish competence and intention, and beyond the mere assertion that education is taking place which Lord Donaldson determined was inadequate.

Many parents are quite concerned not to have their child's privacy invaded out of respect for the child's autonomy, and any hint of testing or examination by strangers with a different agenda can be experienced as undermining. Therefore, for reasons of educational approach, some parents may not wish to provide information to their LEA through home visits.

It would be helpful if LEAs carry out their duty to accept information provided in any reasonable and adequate form, by not making a prior assumption of the normalcy of **any** particular form this might take, but on first approach to present the parents with the free choice the law supports.

In the case of R v Surrey Quarter Sessions Appeals Committee, ex parte Tweedie (1963), Lord Parker held that: *"an education authority should not, as a matter of policy, insist on inspection in the home as the only method of satisfying themselves that the children were receiving full time education".*

There is no legal requirement for the LEA to make continual enquiries. Once in receipt of a reasonable account of the educational provision, their legal obligation is fulfilled and no further contact is necessary. Some parents, however, may appreciate continuous help, support and contact and under these circumstances further contact can be arranged. Some LEAs arrange 'drop-in' centres where families can maintain contact.

School Attendance Orders
Education Act 1996 s 437-443, (previously s 192-198 1993 Act)
This begins:

> *"If it appears to a local education authority that a child of compulsory school age in their area is not receiving suitable education, either by regular attendance at school or otherwise, they shall serve a notice in writing on the parent."*

The formal steps provided for in these sections should not be needed unless something has gone seriously wrong. Nevertheless, they are summarised here for reference:
1. If the LEA has evidence that the educational provision appears to be inadequate, the LEA must serve the parents with a notice giving them at least 15 days to satisfy them that they are educating properly.
2. If the parents fail to do this, the LEA then has to consider whether it is expedient for the child to go to school. If they think it is they must serve a 'school attendance order', but before doing so they must serve a notice stating which school they intend to name in the order, and giving the parents a chance to choose an alternative.
3. The LEA serves a school attendance order requiring the parents to register the child as a pupil at the school named in it.
4. The parents can ask the LEA to revoke the order because they are educating 'otherwise'.
5. The LEA can prosecute the parents for not complying with the order, but the action will fail if the parents can show the court that they are educating 'otherwise'.

The evidence a court requires to satisfy it that adequate education is taking place, is such as would convince **'a reasonable person'**, **'on the balance of probabilities'.** (Under section 447, whether they prosecute or not, the LEA must also consider applying for an education supervision order.)

Diverse approaches to home education

The principle of parental choice is paramount. Families are entitled to choose what they feel to be the most suitable educational approach.

One system cannot be expected to cater for the needs and interests of all individuals. Many fail to thrive or reach their full potential whilst receiving formal instruction in a school environment. A variety of alternatives in education is therefore important **and the law allows for this diversity.**

A clearer interpretation of some terminology used in the 1944 Education Act, (replaced by the 1996 Act), was gained in the case of Harrison & Harrison v Stephenson, (appeal to Worcester Crown Court 1981). The term **'suitable education'** was defined as one which enabled the children 'to achieve their full potential', and was such as 'to prepare the children for life in modern civilised society'. The term **'efficient'** was defined as achieving 'that which it sets out to achieve'.

Clearly this definition covers a great variety of educational approaches.

There is no one 'correct' educational system. All children learn in different ways and at varying rates, and chronological age has little bearing on the process. It would be wholly inappropriate, for example, to seek to impose 'reading and numeracy age' scales on home-educated children, not subject to the specific educational methods in state schools. Individual children come to literacy and numeracy over a huge age range, which has no subsequent bearing on their competence in these areas as adults. **It is vital that parents and children choose a type of education which is right for them, and it is important that any LEA officers understand and are supportive of many differing approaches or 'ways of educating' which are all feasible and legally valid.**

Education Act 1996, Part V (incorporating Education Reform Act 1988)

This deals with the National Curriculum, stating in ss 351 to 353 (replacing ss1&2) that it applies only to children who are registered pupils of maintained, (i.e. State or State-supported), schools.

Home educators may choose whether to base their studies around these guidelines fully, partially, or not at all.

Irregular or non-attendance at school
Education Act 1996 s 444, (previously s 199 of 1993 Act derived from s 39 1944 Act).

This deals with the non-attendance, or irregular attendance at school, of registered pupils. If poor/non-attendance is due to severe school anxieties, usually the Educational Welfare Department becomes involved **and the family should be informed of all their duties, rights and available options including education at home.**

Many LEAs, when confronted with the problems of School Phobia/Anxieties, School Refusal/Truanting, encourage families to contact one of the home education support groups for help and advice. This provides a useful alternative course of action for officials, because if endeavours are made to pressure children with the above problems back into schools under duress, the whole family, (as well as the child), suffers the ensuing stress and the truanting and nervous illnesses inevitably continue. **Education at home may prevent further distress and the possibility of the child returning to school at a later date remains an option.**

Flexi-time or part-time schooling
There may be families who would prefer a flexi-time schooling approach.

Under s 444(3)(a) of the 1996 Education Act,

> *"Any 'school age' child who goes to school at all must attend regularly, but absence 'with leave' does not count as irregular attendance. During such absences the child is officially at school, but is effectively being educated off site. She/he is therefore covered for insurance and attracts full funding. Such arrangements are at the discretion of the school." (s 444 (9))*

Home educating children with Special Educational Needs.
Children with special educational needs, (SEN), are defined in section 312 (1) of the 1996 Education Act as having:
> *"a learning difficulty which calls for special educational provision to be made for him."*

A 'learning difficulty' is further defined with regard to children over 5 in section 312 (2):
> *"(a) he has a significantly greater difficulty in learning than the majority of children of his age,*
> *(b) he has a disability which either prevents or hinders him from making use of educational facilities of a kind generally provided for children of his age in schools within the area of the local education authority..."*

The right to home educate children with SEN is upheld by section 7 (b) :

> *"The parent of every child of compulsory school age shall cause him to receive efficient full-time education suitable ;*
> *a) to his age, ability, and aptitude, and*
> ***b) to any special educational needs he may have,***
> *either by regular attendance at school **or otherwise.**"*

No particular qualifications or special needs training are required of parents fulfilling their Section 7 duty by educating 'otherwise'.

Section 313 (2) of the Act gives LEAs a duty to have regard to the provision of The Code of Practice on the Identification and Assessment of Special Educational Needs, issued by the secretary of State.

Identification and assessment of children with SEN

Section 321 (3) (d) states that, in the area of SEN only, LEAs 'are responsible for' a child :

> *"if he is in their area and ... he is not a registered pupil at a school but is not under the age of two or over compulsory school age and has been brought to their attention as having (or probably having) SEN."*

Under section 321 (2) LEAs have a duty formally to **identify** a child for whom they are responsible **if:**

> *"(a) he has special educational needs, **and***
> ***(b) it is necessary for the authority to determine the special educational provision which any learning difficulty he may have calls for."***

Although the LEA have a responsibility toward home-educated children with special educational needs, in their area, they would only need **formally** to identify and assess those children if the authority themselves needed to make provision for those special educational needs. Where the parents and the LEA are satisfied that the needs can be catered for by the parents in a home-based education, embarking on the formal assessment and statementing procedure should not be necessary.

Statements of SEN

The statementing procedure is primarily designed to facilitate the LEA in deciding what special educational provision it may need to make beyond that being provided by a school or family.

Section 324 (1) states that:

> *"If, in the light of an assessment under section 323 ... it is necessary for the local educational authority to determine the special educational provision which any learning difficulty he*

> *may have calls for, the authority shall make and maintain a statement of his special educational needs."*

If an LEA carries out a statutory assessment of a child educated otherwise and conclude that the child's special educational needs cannot be met without extra funding by the LEA or that it would be beneficial for the LEA to monitor the child's progress, a statement must be made. The LEA must first serve the parent with a proposed statement, (Schedule 27 (2) (a)). A parent may, within certain time restraints, appeal against any part of the proposed statement. The LEA may also decide that a statement will not be necessary. In such cases they must give notice in writing of the decision and of the parent's right to appeal, (section 325 (1)).

The SEN Code of Practice section 4.18 states that the LEA should also consider issuing a 'note in lieu of a statement', against which a parent wanting a statement may also appeal.

The LEA has a duty to honour the rights of parents to make representations, to request reassessment and to appeal to the Special Educational Needs Tribunal as detailed in sections 326 and 328 and Schedule 27 of the 1996 Act, and to inform fully the parent of those rights.

Where issue of a statement is necessary and an LEA is to make provision for the child's special educational needs, section 319 of the Act allows for the provision to be made by the LEA **otherwise than in a school.**

Maintenance of a statement
When a statement is issued, for as long as it is in place, the LEA has a duty to maintain it and to review the statement and provision for the child's special educational needs, annually. The Code of Practice 1994 section 6:1 also allows for the LEA to review the statement at any other time.

At review, the statement of a child who is de-registered from school, for the purposes of education 'otherwise' may need amendment, particularly:

• Where section 4 of the statement names a particular school or type of facility it will need to be altered to education otherwise than at school.

• It may be clear to the parent and the LEA that some of the special provision can now readily be provided by the parent.

At review, it may be possible to cease the statement of a child educated 'otherwise'.

- The child may no longer need extra provision once out of the school environment
- It may be clear to the parent and the LEA that all of the special provision can readily be provided by the parent without LEA oversight.

Further reading

A detailed account of the law and home education further qualifying the points made throughout this document, can be found in *Home Education and the Law* (1991) by Dr. David Deutsch & Kolya Wolf, which has been subject to careful checking by a solicitor and by Counsel's Opinion, to ensure *that, "all statements of law, regulations and proper legal and administrative practice that it contains are correct".* (Preface to 2nd Edition).
(3rd edition due for publication autumn 1999)

Deutsch & Wolf observe that :

> *"It was never the intention of Parliament to compel all children to attend school. Nor was it ever the intention to specify, or to empower LEAs to specify, the form and content of every child's education. Parents who wish to provide a 'proper education' for their children otherwise than at school cannot legally be prevented from doing so ...., and parents do not need to obtain permission or approval from anyone .... "* (Pg.3)

> *"... There exist many contending educational philosophies, giving rise to many different styles of education which are reasonable even though they differ radically amongst themselves ... The issue is not whether the education is approved of or disapproved of by the LEA or by anyone else."* (Pg.6)

> *"Both among experts and among laymen there is no unanimous agreement as to what constitutes a proper education ... "* (Pg.6)

The document contained in this appendix is the work of a large number of home educators including, but not exclusively, members of 'Education Otherwise' *and* 'Choice in Education'. *It was edited by Neil Taylor, and checked for legal accuracy by a team of home educating lawyers.*

Free copying and distribution of this document, unaltered and in its entirety, is encouraged. Authenticity of the original can be verified by the editor.

Further paper copies in A4 sheet (for easy photocopying), or A5 booklet form are available from **'Choice in Education'**, *an independent publication for Home Educators,*
PO Box 20284, London, NW1 3WY

£1.00 for A4, and £0.75p per copy for A5 to cover printing, post and packing costs.

It is also available free on-line in a choice of formats at:
http://www.btinternet.com/~choiceineducation/guidelines.htm

Appendix 2

The questions below are those which were used to gather information from parents and children following an autonomous approach. Thanks are due to all those families who took the time to reply.

1. Given that you advocate an autonomous style of education, how would you personally define 'education'?

2. What theories of education do you use to support your decisions to educate autonomously?

3. How do you deal with the popular theory that certain 'essentials' need to be taught?

4. How would you answer the criticism that autonomous education will not lead to a 'balanced' education?

5. What factors do you see as 'helpful' and 'harmful' in enabling children to learn?

6. What effects do you perceive autonomous education having on children's ability to socialise and negotiate with people outside of the immediate family?

7. There is a common misconception that autonomy in education is permissive and/or neglectful and leads to children who are selfish, demanding, uncooperative, etc. How would you address these impressions?

8. In what ways do you see autonomous education effecting the overall lifestyle of a home educating family?

9. Do issues of autonomous education effect your stance on parenting, e.g. should autonomy extend to issues such as bedtime, television viewing, chores, meal times, etc. and how do you see these freedoms relating to the learning process?

10. If you do not monitor and evaluate children's progress how could you know that learning is taking place?

11. If called upon to give evidence of education to a local education authority, (or other relevant school/education authority), what, in your view, would constitute reasonable evidence and still be in keeping with the principles of autonomous education?

12. How do you see autonomous education enabling children to take ongoing opportunities for higher education and fit into the world of work?

13. Please add any general reflections on autonomous education - why you believe this to be the best method of education, any other criticisms you have encountered and how you feel they should be answered etc.

References and further reading

Aldort, Naomi, *Natural Child Project* web-site at www.naturalchild.com

Caruso, Denise (1999) *Linking entertainment to violence*, NewYork Times, 26th April 1999

Deutsch, David & Wolf, Kolya (1991) *Home Education & the Law,* See also TCS web-site at www.tcs.ac

Gatto, John, articles from the UK Home Education Conference for 2000 and beyond can now be found on the *Choice in Education* web-site at www.choiceineducation.co.uk

Gatto, John (1992) *Dumbing us down,* Philadephia: New Society Publishers

Godwin, William (1970) *The Enquirer*, Kelley

Goldberg, Bruce (1960) *Why Schools Fail,* Cato Institute

Holt, John (1990) *How Children Fail,* Harmondsworth: Penguin

Holt, John (1981) *Teach Your Own*, Lighthouse Books

Illich, Ivan (1971) *Deschooling Society,* Harper & Row

Jackson, Deborah (1990) *Three in a Bed*, Bloomsbury

Jackson, Deborah (1994) *Do not Disturb,* Bloomsbury

Kohn, Alfie (1995) *Punished by Rewards,* Houghton Mifflin

Lawrence, Sarah, articles in *Taking Children Seriously,* paper journal and web-site at www.tcs.ac

Liedlof, Jean (1989) *The Continuum Concept,* Arkana

Meighan, Roland, articles from *Natural Parent* magazine can be found on Educational Heretics web-site at www.gn.apc.org/edheretics/

Meighan, Roland (1997) *The Next Learning System: and why home-schoolers are trailblazers*, Nottingham: Educational Heretics Press

Miller, Alice (1987) *For Your Own Good,* London: Virago

Priesnitz, Wendy *Child's Play*, The Alternate Press, now at www.life.ca/index.html

Popper, Karl (1995) *The Myth of the Framework,* Routledge

Popper, Karl (1995) *In Search of a Better World*, Routledge

Szasz, Thomas (1970) 'Mental Health Services in the Schools', from *Ideology & Insanity*, Doubleday Anchor

Vidal-Hall et al., *To Be Free*, journal of Libertarian Family Network

Webb, Julie (1999*) Those Unschooled Minds: home-educated children grown up*, Nottingham: Educational Heretics Press

Educational Heretics Press is a not-for-profit organisation devoted to *"questioning the dogmas of education in general and schooling in particular"*, with a view to developing the logistics of the next, more humane and effective, learning system.

Those unschooled minds:
home-educated children grow up
by Julie Webb

The book is based on interviews with 20 home educated people. They are now in their twenties or thirties except for one, a man who older. Julie Webb first spoke to about a quarter of them as teenagers in the early 1980s. She wanted to find out what sort of lives they were leading now, and hear their reflections on the process of home educating - she thought it would be interesting to see whether they would contemplate home educating their own children. She hopes her discussion of interviewees' reflections on their experiences will shed an incidental light on the growth of a movement with some fairly revolutionary implications for standard educational thinking.

The people who are the subject of Julie's book, home educated for part or all of their years of compulsory education, come from families with many different reasons for ditching the orthodox structure. The common factor in their approach is the intention of replacing the *"one size fits all"* philosophy, with learning that emerges from the abilities and interests of the individual, deepening and expanding as the child matures.

ISBN   1-900219-15-8   Price £9-95

The Next Learning System:
and why home-schoolers are trailblazers
by Roland Meighan

"I started reading it at 10 o'clock at night and I could not put it down until I had finished it, so you cost me some sleep ..."
Colin Rose, Director, Accelerated Learning Systems

"Any one who takes a look at our educational system knows that it must change profoundly. We need fundamental re-thinking, not just fiddling about with he existing pattern of things - often in autocratic and destructive ways. Aptly, into this situation, comes Roland Meighan's new book, *The Next Learning System*. It sets down the reasons for change, the patterns for change, and it hones in on the dynamics of the learning mind."
Dr. James Hemming

ISBN   1-900219-04-2   £7-95

Other books by Educational Heretics Press

A.S.Neill:'bringing happiness to some few chidren' £8-95

John Holt (paperback at £10-95) (hardback at £17-95)

Edmond Holmes: the tragedy of education' £7-95

Margaret McMillan: 'I learn, to succour the helpless' £7-95

Alice Miller: unkind society, parenting, schooling £7-95

Robert Owen: 'schooling the innocents' £7-95

The Next Learning System:
and why home-schoolers are trailblazers £7-95

Rules Routines and Regimentation:
young children reporting on their schooling £8-95

Participation, Power-sharing and
School Improvement £9-95

Parenting Without God:
experiences of a Humanist mother £7-95

Finding Voices, Making Choices:
the Communty Arts Workers £9-95

The Holistic Educators £7-95

Small Schools and Democratic Practice £7-95

Compulsory Schooling Disease £6-95

Theory and Practice of Regressive Education £7-95

Freethinkers' Guide to the Educational Universe
(Collection of quotations on education) £12-50

Freethinkers' Pocket Directory to the Educational
Universe £7-95

Educational Heretics Press
113 Arundel Drive, Bramcote Hills, Nottingham NG9 3FQ
(For a catalogue, phone 0115 925 7261)